Focus on Grammar

A **BASIC** Course for Reference and Practice

VOLUME A

Focus on Grammar

A **BASIC** Course for Reference and Practice

SECOND EDITION

Irene E. Schoenberg

For Harris, Dan, and Dahlia

Focus on Grammar: A **Basic** Course for Reference and Practice

Pearson Education, 10 Bank Street, White Plains, NY 10606

Editorial director: Allen Ascher
Executive editor: Louisa Hellegers
Director of design and production: Rhea Banker
Development editor: Carolyn Viola-John
Production manager: Alana Zdinak
Managing editor: Linda Moser
Senior production editor: Virginia Bernard
Production editor: Christine Lauricella
Senior manufacturing manager: Patrice Fraccio
Manufacturing supervisor: David Dickey
Photo research: Matthew McConnochie and Marianne Carello
Cover design: Rhea Banker
Cover image: *Elm, Middleton Woods, Yorkshire,*
    6 November 1980. Copyright © Andy Goldsworthy
    from his book *A Collaboration with Nature,*
    Harry N. Abrams, 1990.
Text design: Charles Yuen
Text composition: Preface, Inc.
Illustrators: Ronald Chironna: pp. 10, 83, 119, 165, 170, 171, 184, 185, 200; Jock MacRae: pp. 63, 158,
    161; Paul McCusker: pp. 52, 53, 62, 67, 73, 121, 129, 174, 188, 199, 207, 222; Dusan Petricic: pp. 11,
    25, 30, 41, 98, 108, 120, 190, 201, 211; Dave Sullivan: pp. 1, 2, 3, 5, 8, 9, 12, 14, 15, 16, 19, 22, 23,
    24, 27, 38, 39, 40, 44, 46, 51, 53, 55, 58, 59, 68, 70, 78, 78, 82, 93, 96, 106, 112, 113, 118, 119, 122,
    126, 131, 133, 134, 136, 139, 140, 148, 162, 166, 182, 188, 193, 197, 208.
Photo credits: see p. xiv

ISBN 0-201-34689-3

8 9 10—CRK—07 06 05

CONTENTS

INTRODUCTION   ix

PART I

THE VERB *BE*: PRESENT AND PAST   2
The Mystery of Rocky

UNIT 1   **THE PRESENT AFFIRMATIVE OF *BE***   4
          A story: *Milt's a detective.*

UNIT 2   **THE PRESENT NEGATIVE OF *BE***   12
          Thoughts: *My work is not easy.*

UNIT 3   **THE PRESENT OF *BE*: YES / NO QUESTIONS**   19
          A conversation: *Are you new here?*

UNIT 4   **THE PAST TENSE OF *BE*; PAST TIME MARKERS**   27
          A thank you note: *You were wonderful.*

REVIEW OR SELFTEST   33

FROM GRAMMAR TO WRITING: CAPITALIZATION—Writing a postcard   35

PART II

NOUNS, ADJECTIVES, AND PREPOSITIONS;   38
THE PRESENT PROGRESSIVE
Wonderful Sons, Lucky Daughters-in-law

UNIT 5   **COUNT NOUNS; *A / AN***   40
          A conversation: *My grandson is a chef and an athlete.*

UNIT 6   **DESCRIPTIVE ADJECTIVES**   46
          A thank you note: *The cookies are delicious.*

UNIT 7   **PREPOSITIONS OF PLACE**   51
          A visit to the eye doctor: *The W is between the Q and the Z.*

UNIT 8   **PRESENT PROGRESSIVE**   55
          A telephone conversation: *Pete's doing the laundry.*

REVIEW OR SELFTEST   64

FROM GRAMMAR TO WRITING: SUBJECTS AND VERBS—Writing about people   66

PART III

WH- QUESTIONS; POSSESSIVES; PREPOSITIONS OF TIME   68
The Winston Family

UNIT 9   **QUESTIONS WITH *WHO*, *WHAT*, AND *WHERE***   70
          A visit: *What's a secret?*

UNIT 10   **POSSESSIVE NOUNS AND POSSESSIVE ADJECTIVES; QUESTIONS WITH *WHOSE***   78
          A class discussion: *Whose composition is this?*

UNIT 11   **QUESTIONS WITH *WHEN* AND *WHAT* + NOUN;**   85
          PREPOSITIONS; ORDINAL NUMBERS
          School holidays: *When is Election Day?*

UNIT 12   QUESTIONS WITH *WHO, WHOM,* AND *WHY;*   92
WH- QUESTIONS AND THE PRESENT PROGRESSIVE
A telephone conversation: *Why is Lulu watching TV in bed?*

REVIEW OR SELFTEST   100

FROM GRAMMAR TO WRITING: PUNCTUATION I: THE APOSTROPHE, THE COMMA,   102
THE PERIOD, THE QUESTION MARK—Interviewing and writing about
a classmate

PART IV

THE SIMPLE PRESENT TENSE   106
Clothes for a Teenager

UNIT 13   SIMPLE PRESENT TENSE: AFFIRMATIVE AND NEGATIVE STATEMENTS   108
A letter to a psychologist: *My son loves clothes.*

UNIT 14   SIMPLE PRESENT TENSE: *YES / NO* QUESTIONS AND SHORT ANSWERS   116
A roommate questionnaire: *Do you listen to loud music?*

UNIT 15   SIMPLE PRESENT TENSE: *WH-* QUESTIONS   122
Night owls and early birds: *What time do you get up?*

UNIT 16   SIMPLE PRESENT TENSE AND *THIS / THAT / THESE / THOSE*   131
Cleaning a closet: *This is my favorite sweater.*

UNIT 17   SIMPLE PRESENT TENSE AND *ONE / ONES* AND *IT*   136
Borrowing clothes: *There are two big ones and one small one.*

REVIEW OR SELFTEST   142

FROM GRAMMAR TO WRITING: TIME WORD CONNECTORS—Writing about   145
a routine

PART V

THE SIMPLE PAST TENSE   148
The Winstons' Thanksgiving Day

UNIT 18   SIMPLE PAST TENSE: REGULAR VERBS—AFFIRMATIVE AND
NEGATIVE STATEMENTS   150
A postcard: *Last night we walked along the Seine River.*

UNIT 19   SIMPLE PAST TENSE: IRREGULAR VERBS—AFFIRMATIVE AND
NEGATIVE STATEMENTS   158
A Chinese folktale: *He always said, "You never know what will happen."*

UNIT 20   SIMPLE PAST TENSE: *YES / NO* AND *WH-* QUESTIONS   165
Lost and found: *What did Norma lose?*

REVIEW OR SELFTEST   176

FROM GRAMMAR TO WRITING: PUNCTUATION II: THE EXCLAMATION POINT,   179
THE HYPHEN, QUOTATION MARKS—Writing a story you heard as a child

PART VI

IMPERATIVES; SUGGESTIONS; *THERE IS / THERE ARE*   182
Let's Stop for Pizza

UNIT 21   IMPERATIVES; SUGGESTIONS WITH *LET'S, WHY DON'T WE . . .?;*   184
WHY DON'T YOU . . .?
Person in the news: Luigi Paolini: *Why don't we step into my office?*

UNIT 22   SUBJECT AND OBJECT PRONOUNS; DIRECT AND INDIRECT OBJECTS   193
A conversation: *It's my yutaka. My mom sent it to me last month.*

UNIT 23   THERE IS / THERE ARE / IS THERE . . .? / ARE THERE . . .?   201
Shopping malls: *Is there a mall around here?*

UNIT 24   NUMBERS, QUANTIFIERS, AND QUESTIONS WITH HOW MANY . . .?   208
Complaints: *How many do you want?*

REVIEW OR SELFTEST   215

FROM GRAMMAR TO WRITING: SENTENCE COMBINING WITH AND AND BUT—   219
Describing a street

APPENDICES

APPENDIX 1   Map of the World   A-0—A-1

APPENDIX 2   Map of the United States and Canada   A-2

APPENDIX 3   Numbers, Temperature, Months, Days, Seasons, Titles   A-3—A-4

APPENDIX 4   Time   A-4

APPENDIX 5   Parts of the Body; Medical Problems   A-5

APPENDIX 6   Holidays in the United States and Canada   A-6

APPENDIX 7   Plural Nouns: Spelling and Pronunciation Rules   A-7—A-8

APPENDIX 8   Possessive Nouns   A-8

APPENDIX 9   Non-count Nouns and Names of Containers   A-9

APPENDIX 10   The Definite Article   A-10

APPENDIX 11   Verb Tenses   A-11—A-12

APPENDIX 12   Base Forms and Past-Tense Forms of Common Irregular Verbs   A-13

APPENDIX 13   The Present Progressive: Spelling Rules   A-13

APPENDIX 14   The Simple Present Tense: Spelling and Pronunciation Rules A-14

APPENDIX 15   The Simple Past Tense: Spelling and Pronunciation Rules   A-15

APPENDIX 16   Comparisons with Adjectives and Adverbs   A-16

APPENDIX 17   Modals   A-17

APPENDIX 18   Pronunciation Table   A-18

INDEX

I-1

ABOUT THE AUTHOR

Irene E. Schoenberg has taught ESL for over twenty-five years at Hunter College's *International English Language Institute* and for eighteen years at Columbia University's *American Language Program*. She has trained ESL and EFL teachers at the New School for Social Research and has lectured at conferences and English language schools and universities in Brazil, Mexico, Thailand, Taiwan, Japan, and the United States. She is the author of ***Talk about Trivia*** and ***Talk about Values*** and co-author of the ***True Colors*** series with Jay Maurer. Ms. Schoenberg holds an MA in TESOL from Columbia University. ***Focus on Grammar: A Basic Course for Reference and Practice*** has grown out of the author's experience as a practicing teacher of English.

AUTHOR'S GOAL AND PURPOSE

In writing *Focus on Grammar*: *A Basic Course for Reference and Practice*, I have tried to avoid presenting grammar divorced from practical use. It has been my pleasure in the classroom and my goal here to integrate grammar into informative and amusing units which, because they reflect real life, will motivate students to learn and use English. I hope this material will provide your students with as much pleasure and confidence with grammar as it has mine.

INTRODUCTION

THE **FOCUS ON GRAMMAR** SERIES

Focus on Grammar: A Basic Course for Reference and Practice, Second Edition, is the first text in the four-level **Focus on Grammar** series. Written by practicing ESL professionals, the series focuses on English grammar through lively listening, speaking, reading, and writing activities. Each of the four Student Books is accompanied by an Answer Key, a Workbook, an Audio Program (cassettes or CDs), a Teacher's Manual, and a CD–ROM. Each Student Book can stand alone as a complete text in itself, or it can be used as part of the series.

BOTH CONTROLLED AND COMMUNICATIVE PRACTICE

Research in applied linguistics suggests that students expect and need to learn the formal rules of a language. However, students need to practice new structures in a variety of contexts to help them internalize and master them. To this end, **Focus on Grammar** provides an abundance of both controlled and communicative exercises so that students can bridge the gap between knowing grammatical structures and using them. The many communicative activities in each unit enable students to personalize what they have learned in order to talk to each other with ease about hundreds of everyday issues.

A UNIQUE FOUR-STEP APPROACH

The series follows a unique four-step approach. In the first step, **grammar in context,** new structures are shown in the natural context of conversations, and narratives. This is followed by a **grammar presentation** of structures in clear and accessible grammar charts, notes, and examples. The third step is **focused practice** of both form and meaning in numerous and varied controlled exercises with objective answers. In the fourth step, **communication practice,** students use the new structures freely and creatively in motivating, open-ended activities.

A COMPLETE CLASSROOM TEXT AND REFERENCE GUIDE

A major goal in the development of **Focus on Grammar** has been to provide Student Books that serve not only as vehicles for classroom instruction but also as resources for reference and self-study. In each Student Book, the combination of grammar charts, grammar notes, and expansive appendices provides a complete and invaluable reference guide for the student. And exercises in the focus practice sections of each unit are also ideal for individual study.

THOROUGH RECYCLING

Underpinning the scope and sequence of the series as a whole is the belief that students need to use target structures many times in many contexts at increasing levels of difficulty. For this reason new grammar is constantly recycled so that students will feel thoroughly comfortable with it.

COMPREHENSIVE TESTING PROGRAM

SelfTests at the end of each part of the Student Book allow for continual assessment of progress. In addition, diagnostic and final tests in the Teacher's Manual provide a ready-made, ongoing evaluation component for each student.

THE **BASIC** STUDENT BOOK

Focus on Grammar: A Basic Course for Reference and Practice, *Second Edition,* is written for the beginning and false beginning student. Activities take both levels into account and allow students to demonstrate their ability at different levels.

ORGANIZATION

This book is divided into eleven parts comprising forty-four units. A final section called *Putting It All Together* reviews the major structures of the book. Each of the eleven parts begins with a preview that incorporates the grammar of the part into a lighthearted conversation. Though the characters in the preview are featured throughout the book, parts or units can be studied in any order, allowing the instructor to tailor this text to his or her particular class. Each unit contains the four sections that comprise the essence of *Focus on Grammar:* Grammar in Context, Grammar Presentation, Focused Practice, and Communication Practice. A Review or SelfTest (with answers) and a From Grammar to Writing section conclude each part.

PREVIEW

The preview presents the grammar of the entire part in a natural context. An important belief of the *Focus on Grammar* series is that grammar is an aid to the meaningful use of language. Since students usually understand the meaning of a structure before they master its use, they begin by reading and listening to a conversation that includes the new grammar structures. This initial introduction makes it easier for students to then understand and use grammar appropriately. It also helps them realize that the grammar focus is a means to an end, the end being the appropriate use of the structure in a natural context.

GRAMMAR IN CONTEXT

Grammar in Context presents the grammar of the unit in a natural setting. The texts, all of which are recorded, present language in various formats.

These include telephone conversations, letters, questionnaires, radio talk shows, quiz shows, folktales, essays, and conversations among friends and relatives. In addition, the introductory sections motivate students and provide an opportunity for incidental learning and lively classroom discussion. Topics include a mystery, a discussion of the role of women, a letter to a psychologist, the problems of perfectionists, a matchmaker's questions, suggestions for public speaking, and the use of white lies. A **Warm Up** precedes each text and gives students a chance to express their thoughts and opinions on the topic.

GRAMMAR PRESENTATION

This section is made up of grammar charts, notes, and examples. The Grammar **charts** focus on the form of the unit's target structure. Clear and easy-to-understand boxes present each grammatical form in all its combinations. These charts provide students with a clear visual reference for each new structure. The Grammar **notes** explain the grammar shown in the preceding chart. These notes give definitions, describe the form, offer distinctions between the spoken and written language, and point out potential problems. Every note includes at least one example, and reference notes provide cross-references to related units and the Appendices.

FOCUSED PRACTICE

This section provides practice of the form and meaning of the structures presented in the Grammar Presentation. In the first exercise, **Discover the Grammar**, students indicate their awareness and recognition of the grammar. After this activity, students do a variety of contextualized exercises that progress from more controlled to more productive. Exercises are cross-referenced to the appropriate grammar notes so that students can review the notes if necessary. In addition, a variety of listening activities provide another dimension in which students can practice and incorporate the target grammar. A complete **Answer Key** is provided in a separate booklet.

COMMUNICATION PRACTICE

The Communication Practice activities give students an opportunity to use the structures in more creative ways, allowing them to express their own thoughts and opinions in pair or group work. Through class surveys, discussions, information gaps, games, value clarifications, and problem solving activities, students gain confidence in the target structure as well as many other structures in the language.

REVIEW OR SELFTEST

After the last unit of each part, there is a review section that can be used as a self-test. The exercises test the form and use of the grammar content of the part. These tests include questions in the format of the Structure and Written Expression sections of the TOEFL®. An **Answer Key** is provided after each test.

FROM GRAMMAR TO WRITING

At the end of each part there is a section that gives students practical information about different aspects of writing such as the rules of punctuation and capitalization, models of business letters or informal letters, and ways to organize a paragraph. Students practice writing short passages that review the structures of the part.

APPENDICES

The appendices provide useful information including current maps, lists of the days, months, numbers, common irregular verbs, common non-count nouns, modals with their meaning and examples, tense form charts, spelling and pronunciation rules of tenses, and a phonetic pronunciation chart.

NEW IN THIS EDITION

In response to users' requests, this edition has:

- a revised table of contents with the introduction of the tenses earlier in the text (allowing students to say more sooner)

- a Grammar in Context and a Warm Up providing a theme and context for every unit

- a new easy-to-read format for grammar notes and examples

- vocabulary enrichment through the grouping of vocabulary items by topics such as occupations, relationships, clothing

- cross-references that link exercises to corresponding grammar notes

- more photos and art

- more listening exercises

- more information gaps

- the inclusion of editing exercises

- a From Grammar to Writing section at the end of each part

SUPPLEMENTARY COMPONENTS

All supplementary components of *Focus on Grammar, Second Edition,* —the Audio Program (cassettes or CDs), the Workbook, and the Teacher's Manual—are tightly keyed to the Student Book. Along with the CD-ROM, these components provide a wealth of practice and an opportunity to tailor the series to the needs of each individual classroom.

AUDIO PROGRAM

All of the Preview conversations as well as the Grammar in Context passages and many of the Focus practice exercises are recorded on cassettes and CDs. These include clozes, task-based listening, and pronunciation exercises. The symbol ▇ appears next to these activities. The scripts appear in the Teacher's Manual and may be used as an alternative way of presenting these activities.

WORKBOOK

The Workbook accompanying *Focus on Grammar: A Basic Course for Reference and Practice, Second Edition,* provides a wealth of additional exercises appropriate for self-study of the target grammar of each unit in the Student Book. These exercises follow the sequence of the unit. This enables the instructor to make daily homework assignments or allows the instructor to work with individuals or small groups while students are doing the exercises.

TEACHER'S MANUAL

The Teacher's Manual, divided into five parts, contains a variety of suggestions and information to enrich the material in the Student Book. The first part gives general suggestions for each section of a typical unit. The next part offers practical teaching suggestions and cultural information to accompany specific material in each unit. The Teacher's Manual also provides ready-to-use diagnostic and final tests for each of the eleven parts of the Student Book. In addition, a complete script of the audio program is provided, as is an answer key for the diagnostic and final tests.

CD-ROM

The *Focus on Grammar* CD-ROM provides individualized practice with immediate feedback. Fully contextualized and interactive, the activities broaden and extend practice of the grammatical structures in the reading, listening, and writing skill areas. The CD-ROM includes grammar review, review tests, and all relevant reference material from the Student Book. It can also be used alongside the *Longman Interactive American Dictionary* CD-ROM.

CREDITS

PHOTOGRAPHS

Grateful acknowledgment is given to the following for providing photographs:

p. 4 Courtesy of Oregon State University; **p. 10 (Celine Dion)** AP/Wide World Photos; **p. 10 (Arnold Schwarzenegger)** AP/Wide World Photos; **p. 10 (Leonardo DiCaprio)** © Armando Gallo/Retna; **p. 10 (Prince William)** CORBIS/AFP ©; **p. 10 (Romario)** AP/Wide World Photos; **p. 40** PhotoDisc, Inc.; **p. 50** © TSM/DiMaggio/Kalish; **p. 50** TSM/Alan Schein, 1998; **p. 60** Courtesy of Mrs. Duane Hanson, © 1997; **p. 75** PhotoDisc, Inc.; **p. 85** PhotoEdit; **p. 85** Tony Stone Images; **p. 85** CORBIS/Stephanie Maze ©; **p. 92 ("Seinfeld")** Photofest; **p. 92 (Football)** AP/Wide World Photos; **p. 92 ("E.R.")** Sygma Photo News; **p. 92 (Interview)** Richard A. Bloom; **p. 92 (Murder She Wrote)** Photofest; **p. 92 (Mariah Carey)** SIPA Press; **p. 93** Photos International/Archive Photos; **p. 98** ©Archive Photos; **p. 122** Omni-Photo Communications, Inc.; **p. 128** "Lizard Waiting" by Chad Johnstone. © Tobwabba Art, 1998; **p. 130** CORBIS; **p. 130** Tony Stone Images; **p. 130** PhotoEdit; **p. 173** CORBIS/Burnstein Collection ©; **p. 189** © TSM/Alan Schein, 1998; **p. 201** Tony Stone Images

THE STORY BEHIND THE COVER

The photograph on the cover is the work of **Andy Goldsworthy**, an innovative artist who works exclusively with natural materials to create unique outdoor sculpture, which he then photographs. Each Goldsworthy sculpture communicates the artist's own "sympathetic contact with nature" by intertwining forms and shapes structured by natural events with his own creative perspective. Goldsworthy's intention is not to "make his mark on the landscape, but to create a new perception and an evergrowing understanding of the land."

So, too, *Focus on Grammar* takes grammar found in its most natural context and expertly reveals its hidden structure and meaning. It is our hope that students everywhere will also develop a new perception and an evergrowing understanding of the world of grammar.

ACKNOWLEDGMENTS

As a mother, I know never to compare my children. But as an author preparing a second edition I know that everyone will compare it with the first. For that reason I not only have relied on my own teaching experience with the book, but have also sought the reaction of colleagues and students to what works best and what does not. For indicating what is most enjoyable and effective, I want to thank my students at the International English Language Institute at Hunter College and readers around the world who have spoken or written to me about *Focus on Grammar: A Basic Course for Reference and Practice.*

My gratitude to the consultants who read the manuscript and offered numerous excellent suggestions: **Marcia Edwards Hijaab**, Virginia Commonwealth University, Richmond; **Kevin McClure**, ELS Language Center, San Francisco; **Tim Rees**, Transworld Schools, Boston; **Allison Rice**, International English Language Institute, Hunter College, New York. I also thank **Ellen Shaw**, University of Nevada, Las Vegas, **Ann Larson**, Oregon State University, Corvallis, and **Fran Golden**, Applied Language Institute, Kansas City, Missouri, for their insightful comments on the first edition.

My developmental editor **Carolyn Viola-John**'s devotion to this new edition has been exemplary, and she has offered creative solutions to the problems we have encountered. I thank **Christine Lauricella** for expertly guiding the book through the production process and **Matt McConnochie** for his work as a photo researcher. I thank **Sammy Eckstut** and **Deborah Gordon** for their apt comments and **Penny Laporte** for her keen awareness of the fine points of grammar. **Joan Saslow**, while not directly involved in this project, nonetheless influenced its outcome with her insights into language learning. I appreciate, too, the thoughtful comments of **Marjorie Fuchs** who helped strengthen the Grammar in Context sections and generously remarked on other aspects of the text.

Finally, a book of this type cannot be published without a talented director. I thank **Louisa Hellegers** for overseeing this project with her natural tact and humor. I appreciate too her always being available to answer any of my concerns.

Since this edition results from the popularity of the first, I want to thank the marketing team. My gratitude to **Anne Boynton-Trigg** and all those who presented this book to programs around the world.

And I want to acknowledge those who had a role in the first edition: **Nancy Perry**, **Penny Laporte**, **Louisa Hellegers**, **Joan Saslow**, **Allen Ascher**, **Alison Rice**, **Michelle Rayvid**, **Carlin Good**, **Pamela McPartland-Fairman**, **Laura T. LeDrean**, **Ellen Rosenfield**, **Cynthia Wiseman**, **Helen Ambrosio**, and **Lisa Hutchins**.

To **Joanne Dresner** who first directed this project, I owe more than words. This book would not have been possible without her initial ideas, support, and enthusiastic encouragement.

In the first edition of Focus on Grammar I wrote that being a parent of teenagers and writing a basic level grammar book are both humbling experiences. Now that my children are no longer teenagers, I seem to have become a bit smarter. I only hope that this is reflected in the second edition. To my family, **Harris**, **Dan**, and **Dahlia**, thank you for your love and support.

I.E.S

THE FIRST DAY OF CLASS

James Belmont is a photography teacher. Lulu is a new student. Listen and read their conversation.

LULU WINSTON:	Is this photography 101?
JAMES BELMONT:	Yes, it is. Please come in. I'm James Belmont.
LULU:	Nice to meet you. I'm Lucille Winston.
JAMES:	Is that W-I-N-S-T-O-N?
LULU:	That's right.
JAMES:	Ah yes. Here it is. And your first name is Lucille?
LULU:	Yes, but please call me Lulu.
JAMES:	Okay. Hello, Lulu. Welcome to class.
LULU:	It's good to be here.

THE ALPHABET

Listen and repeat the letters of the alphabet.

Aa Bb Cc Dd Ee Ff Gg Hh Ii Jj Kk Ll Mm Nn Oo Pp Qq Rr Ss Tt Uu Vv Ww Xx Yy Zz

CONVERSATION PRACTICE

Listen to this conversation. Work with a partner. Practice the conversation. Use your own names.

A: What's your name?

B: Milton Costa, but please call me Milt.

A: Okay, Milt. How do you spell that?

B: M-I-L-T.

A: Nice to meet you.

B: Nice to meet you, too.

Write the names of your classmates in a notebook.

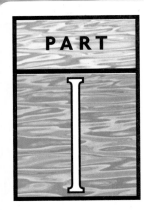
THE VERB *BE:* PRESENT AND PAST

PREVIEW

Pete Winston is in New York, and Milt Costa is in Oregon. Listen and read their telephone conversation.

THE MYSTERY OF ROCKY

MILT: Hello.

PETE: Hi, Milt?

MILT: Yes.

PETE: This is Pete Winston.

MILT: Hi, Pete. How are you? How's business?

PETE: I'm fine, and business is great. But I'm worried.

MILT: Why? What's wrong?

PETE: I'm worried about my daughter Carol.

MILT: Why?

PETE: She's a student at Oregon State University, and she's in love.

MILT: That's wonderful!

PETE: No, it isn't. I don't know her boyfriend.

MILT: Is he a student?

PETE: No, he isn't.

MILT: Is he a teacher?

PETE: No, he isn't.

MILT: What's his name?

PETE: Rocky.

MILT: Rocky?

PETE: Yes, Rocky! Who is this Rocky? Milt, you're an old friend. You're in Oregon now. You're a great detective. Please help me.

MILT: I'll do my best.

PETE: Thanks, Milt. Bye.

MILT: Bye.

SUN WANG: Who was that?

MILT: That was Pete, an old friend.

COMPREHENSION CHECK

Check (✓) **That's right** *or* **That's wrong**.

	That's right.	That's wrong.
1. Pete and Milt are old friends.	✓	☐
2. Pete is worried about his business.	☐	✓
3. Pete is worried about his daughter.	✓	☐
4. Rocky is a student.	☐	✓
5. Milt was not alone.	☐	✓

WITH A PARTNER

Practice the conversation on pages 2 and 3.

THE PRESENT AFFIRMATIVE OF *BE*

GRAMMAR **IN CONTEXT**

WARM UP   Is your school big? Is your school in a big city?

Oregon State University

Corvallis, Oregon

Location: small city

Student population: 15,000

Number of foreign students: 1,200

	Yes	No
1. Oregon State University is a big school.	☑	☐
2. Oregon State University is in a big city.	☐	☑

Milt Costa **is** from Brazil. He **is** in Oregon now. He **is** at Oregon State University. He **is** a detective.

Carol Winston **is** from New York. Yoko Mori **is** from Japan. They **are** new students at Oregon State University. They **are** roommates.

Oregon State University **is** big. It **is** clean and beautiful. The people **are** friendly. It **is** a nice place.

Carol, Yoko, and Yoko's dog **are** with Milt.

GRAMMAR **PRESENTATION**
AFFIRMATIVE STATEMENTS AND CONTRACTIONS WITH *BE*

AFFIRMATIVE STATEMENTS

SINGULAR		
SUBJECT	*BE*	
I	**am**	a student.
You	**are**	happy.
Milt He Carol She	**is**	in the United States.
Oregon It	**is**	a state. beautiful. in the United States.

PLURAL		
SUBJECT	*BE*	
Carol and I We	**are**	students.
You and Carol You Carol and Milt They	**are**	happy. in the United States.
Oregon and New York They	**are**	states. beautiful. in the United States.

CONTRACTIONS

I am	→ **I'm**	we are	→ **we're**
you are	→ **you're**	you are	→ **you're**
he is	→ **he's**	they are	→ **they're**
she is	→ **she's**	Pete is	→ **Pete's**
it is	→ **it's**		

NOTES

1. Every sentence has a subject. The subject is a noun or pronoun. **Subject pronouns** replace **subject nouns**. The subject pronouns are *I, you, he, she, it, we,* and *they.*

EXAMPLES

subject
noun
- **Milt** is a detective.
- **The girls** are students.

subject
pronoun
- **He** is in Oregon.
- **They** are roommates.

2. Every sentence has a verb. The **present tense** of the verb *be* has three forms: *am, are,* and *is*.

- I **am** from Taiwan.
- We **are** doctors.
- It **is** in the United States.

3. Use the verb *be* before **nouns, adjectives,** or **prepositional phrases**.

A noun can be singular (one) or plural (more than one). Plural nouns usually end in **-s**.

singular noun
- He is **a detective**.

plural noun
- They are **friends**.

adjectives
- It is **big**.
- We are **happy**.

prepositional phrases
- Milt is **from Brazil**.
- He is **in Oregon**.

4. Contractions are short forms. Contractions join two words together. Use contractions in speaking and informal writing.

A contraction joins subject pronouns and the verb *be*.

A contraction also joins a singular noun with *is*.

In a contraction, **an apostrophe (')** replaces a letter.

- **I'm** a teacher.
- **You're** from Caracas.
- **She's** in love.
- **It's** a boy!
- **We're** friends.
- **They're** roommates.

- Pete**'s** worried.
- His daughter**'s** in love.

FOCUSED PRACTICE

1 DISCOVER THE GRAMMAR

Read about the Wangs. Underline the subject and circle the verb in each sentence.

The Wangs are my friends. Sun and Nora Wang are teachers at Oregon State University. They are from Taipei in Taiwan. Sun is a biology teacher. Nora is a chemistry teacher. We are good friends and neighbors.

2 STUDENTS AT OREGON STATE   Grammar Notes 1–3

Complete the sentences. Use **am**, **is**, *or* **are**.

1. Oregon ___is___ a state.

2. It ___is___ in the United States.

3. Carol ___is___ in Oregon.

4. Yoko and Carol ___is___ in Oregon.

5. They ___are___ roommates.

6. They ___are___ new students.

7. We ___are___ students.

8. I ___am___ a student.

9. You ___are___ happy.

10. He ___is___ a detective.

❸ MEET THE WANGS

Write contractions.

1. They __They're__ from Taipei.
    (are)

2. Sun __Sun's__ a biology teacher.
    (is)

3. We __we're__ good friends and neighbors.
    (are)

❹ EDITING

Correct the passage. Add the verb **be** *in seven more places.*

This ^is^ my family. They ^are^ in Brazil. This
^is^ my sister Alessandra. She ^is^ a
teacher. This ^is^ my brother Joao. He ^is^
a businessman. My family ^is^ far away,
but thanks to e-mail, we ^are^ close.

COMMUNICATION PRACTICE

5 WHERE ARE THEY FROM?

*Work with a partner. Talk about the people. Match the people, the stamps, and the
coins with the countries they're from.*

EXAMPLES:
Leonardo DiCaprio is from the United States.
Coin O is from Great Britain.

a. Celine Dion **b.** Arnold Schwarzenegger **c.** Leonardo DiCaprio **d.** Prince William **e.** Romario

1. Canada   2. the United States   3. Austria   4. Brazil   5. Great Britain

6 OCCUPATIONS

Check (✔) your occupation and the occupations of people in your family. Tell your partner. Any surprises? Tell the class.

EXAMPLE:

A: My sister's a detective. My uncle Sam is an artist. My mother is a businesswoman. I'm a student.

B: My father is a writer . . .

Occupations

- ☐ a businessman
- ☐ a businesswoman
- ☐ a detective
- ☐ a salesperson
- ☐ a student
- ☐ a teacher
- ☐ other _____

☐ a nurse

☐ a homemaker

☐ a doctor

☐ an athlete

☐ an electrician

☐ an artist

☐ a plumber

☐ a writer

☐ a singer

☐ a carpenter

☐ a lawyer

THE PRESENT NEGATIVE OF *BE*

GRAMMAR **IN CONTEXT**

WARM UP   Do you like mysteries? Is it difficult to be a detective?
What do you think?

Listen and read Milt's thoughts.

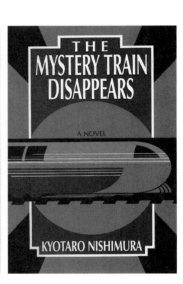

My work **is not** easy. Where is Rocky?
He**'s not** on campus. He**'s not** in the
telephone book. He**'s not** with Carol. Who
is Rocky? He**'s not** a student. He**'s not**
a teacher. Carol's happy, but Pete**'s not**
happy. Pete's worried. But I**'m not**
worried. After all, I'm Milt,
the great detective.

GRAMMAR **PRESENTATION**

NEGATIVE STATEMENTS AND CONTRACTIONS WITH *BE*

SINGULAR	
SUBJECT BE / NOT	
I **am not** I'**m not**	a new teacher. old. from Japan.
You **are not** You'**re not** You **aren't**	
He **is not** He'**s not** He **isn't**	
She **is not** She'**s not** She **isn't**	

PLURAL	
SUBJECT BE / NOT	
We **are not** We'**re not** We **aren't**	teachers. old. from Japan.
You **are not** You'**re not** You **aren't**	
They **are not** They'**re not** They **aren't**	

It **is not** It'**s not** It **isn't**	a state. beautiful. from Japan.

They **are not** They'**re not** They **aren't**	states. beautiful. from Japan.

NOTES	EXAMPLES
1. Use *not* after the verb *be* in negative statements.	• He **is not** a student.
2. There are two ways to make **negative contractions**: Join the subject pronoun and the verb *be*. Join the verb *be* and *not*. ▶ **BE CAREFUL!** There is only one way to make a negative contraction with *I am not*—that is, **I'm not**.	 • You'**re not** old. • You **aren't** old. • I'**m not** an engineer.

FOCUSED PRACTICE

1 DISCOVER THE GRAMMAR

Read Pete's thoughts. Then read the sentences. Check (✓) what's true.

Carol's in Oregon. She's far away. I don't know her boyfriend. He isn't a teacher. He isn't a student. Who is he? I don't know. What's his occupation? I don't know. Milt's a good friend and a good detective, but his work is not easy.

1. Carol is far away. ☑   She isn't far away. ☒
2. Rocky is a teacher. ☒   He isn't a teacher. ☒
3. Milt and Pete are friends. ☑   They aren't friends. ☒
4. Pete's a detective. ☑   He's not a detective. ☒

2 A LETTER   Grammar Notes 1–2

 Listen and read this letter from Milt to his sister. Listen again and complete the sentences. Use **I'm, He's, She's, He's not,** *or* **is not.**

September 8

Hi Alessandra,

_____I'm_____ in Oregon. I'm working for Pete Winston from New York. __He's__
   1.   2.

an old friend. __He's__ a nice man and a great businessman. __He's__ worried
              3.   4.

about his daughter, Carol. __She's__ a new student at Oregon State University.
                          5.

__She's__ in love. Rocky is her boyfriend. __He's not__ a student. __is not__ a
   6.   7.   8.

teacher. Pete __is not__ happy. I want to help him.
             9.

   Write soon. Give my love to the family.

                                             Love,
                                             Milt

---

3 PEOPLE, PLACES, AND OCCUPATIONS — Grammar Notes 1–2

Read the story on page 5. Complete the sentences. Use **'m, 's, 're,** *or* **'m not, isn't,** *or* **aren't.**

1. Yoko ___isn't___ in Japan now. She ___'s___ in Oregon.

2. Carol ___isn't___ from Oregon. She ___'s___ from New York.

3. Milt, Yoko, and Carol ___isn't___ in New York now. They___'re___ in Oregon.

4. Milt ___isn't___ a teacher. He ___'s___ a detective.

5. We___'re___ English teachers. We___'re___ students.

6. I___'m not___ a student. I ___'m___ an English teacher.

7. New York is a city. It ___'s___ a state, too.

4 WHO ARE THEY? — Grammar Notes 1–2

Read the conversation on pages 2 and 3. Complete the sentences. Use the words in the box.

He's, She's	He's not, She's not	They're	They're not

1. ___He's not___ a teacher. ___He's___ a businessman.

2. ___He's___ worried. ___He's not___ relaxed.

3. ___They're___ friends. ___They're not___ cousins.

4. ___He's not___ young. ___He's___ middle-aged.

5. _____ a teacher. _____ a student.

6. _____ from New York. _____ from Oregon.

7. _____ students. _____ detectives.

8. _____ in school. _____ at work.

Now say each negative statement another way. Use contractions.

EXAMPLE:

1. He _____isn't_____ a teacher.

COMMUNICATION PRACTICE

5 DESCRIBING YOURSELF

Check (✓) what is true for you. Read those sentences to a partner.

❑ I'm in love.   ❑ I'm not in love.

❑ I'm a detective.   ❑ I'm not a detective.

❑ I'm a new student.   ❑ I'm not a new student.

❑ I'm worried.   ❑ I'm not worried.

❑ I'm from an old city.   ❑ I'm not from an old city.

❑ I'm busy.   ❑ I'm not busy.

❑ I'm a businessman.   ❑ I'm not a businessman.

❑ I'm an athlete.   ❑ I'm not an athlete.

❑ I'm a plumber.   ❑ I'm not a plumber.

In what ways are you and your partner alike?

EXAMPLE:
We're both new students.

6 THAT'S RIGHT / THAT'S WRONG

Introduce a classmate. Then make true and false statements about your classmate. The class listens and says **That's right** *or* **That's wrong** *and corrects the false statements.*

EXAMPLE:

PABLO: This is Juan Herrera. He's from Colombia. He's a student and an athlete. He's in love.

MARTHA: That's wrong. Juan's not from Colombia. He's from Venezuela.

PABLO: That's right. Juan's from Venezuela.

RICARDO: Juan's not in love.

PABLO: That's wrong. Juan's in love, but it's a secret.

RICARDO: Not anymore!

7 A GEOGRAPHY GAME

Work with a partner. Partner A reads sentences 1–4. Partner B reads sentences 5–8.
*After each sentence, your partner says **That's right** or **That's wrong** and corrects*
the wrong sentences. (See map on pages A-0 and A-1.)

EXAMPLE:
A: São Paulo is in Brazil.
B: That's right.
A: France is in Paris.
B: That's wrong. France isn't in Paris. Paris is in France.

Partner A

1. Great Britain is in Africa.

2. Mongolia is near China.

3. The United States is in Argentina.

4. Australia is near the United States.

Partner B

5. Mali is in Asia.

6. France is not near Spain.

7. Taiwan is near Hong Kong.

8. The United States is in New York.

Now use the map and make more sentences about the world. Your partner
*answers **That's right** or **That's wrong** and corrects the wrong sentences.*

8 THINK ABOUT IT

Work with a partner. Read the sentences and discuss them. Two sentences are
always true. Find them.

EXAMPLE:
A: Detectives are friendly.
B: No, that's not always true.

1. Detectives are friendly.

2. Teachers are women.

3. Taipei and Lima are capital cities.

4. Businessmen are clean.

5. Korea and Colombia are places.

6. New York is clean.

7. Students are happy.

8. Roommates are friends.

9. Washington, D.C. is in Washington.

10. English is easy.

THE PRESENT OF *BE:*
YES / NO QUESTIONS

GRAMMAR **IN CONTEXT**

WARM UP   What do you think? Is the first day of school difficult for new students? Is it difficult for new teachers?

It is the first day of school. Yoko and Al Brown are outside an English class. Listen and read their conversation.

YOKO: Excuse me. **Am I** late for class? **Is the teacher** here?

AL BROWN: **No**, **you're on time**. And **yes, the teacher is here.**

YOKO: Oh, good. I'm Yoko Mori. **Are you new here**?

AL BROWN: **Yes, I am**.

YOKO: I am, too. What's your name?

AL BROWN: Al Brown. Where are you from, Yoko?

YOKO: I'm from Japan. What about you?

AL BROWN: I'm from Michigan.

YOKO: Michigan? Then you're not a new student in this English class.

AL BROWN: You're right. I'm not a new student. I'm a new teacher. I'm *your* new teacher.

GRAMMAR **PRESENTATION**
YES / NO QUESTIONS AND SHORT ANSWERS WITH *BE*

YES / NO QUESTIONS

SINGULAR		
BE	SUBJECT	
Am	I	
Are	you	
	he	from Mexico?
Is	she	
	it	

PLURAL		
BE	SUBJECT	
	we	
Are	you	from Mexico?
	they	

SHORT ANSWERS

SINGULAR			
	YES		*NO*
	you **are**.		you**'re not**. you **aren't**.
	I **am**.		I**'m not**.
Yes,	he **is**.	**No,**	he**'s not**. he **isn't**.
	she **is**.		she**'s not**. she **isn't**.
	it **is**.		it**'s not**. it **isn't**.

PLURAL			
	YES		*NO*
	you **are**.		you**'re not**. you **aren't**.
Yes,	we **are**.	**No,**	we**'re not**. we **aren't**.
	they **are**.		they**'re not**. they **aren't**.

OTHER SHORT ANSWERS

I don't know.
Yes, I think so.
No, I don't think so.

NOTES	EXAMPLES
1. In **questions**, a form of **be** comes before the subject.	subject • **Am** I happy?
2. We usually answer *yes / no* questions with short answers.	**A:** Are you from Korea? **B: Yes.** OR **Yes, I am.**
▶ **BE CAREFUL!** Don't use contractions for short answers with *yes*.	**A:** Are they students? **B: Yes, they are.** NOT ~~Yes, they're.~~
3. We sometimes answer questions with long answers.	**A:** Are they students? **B: Yes, they are students.** OR **Yes, they're students.**
4. When we are unsure of an answer, we say, **"I don't know."** When we think something is true, we say, **"Yes, I think so."** When we think something is untrue, we say **"No, I don't think so."**	**A:** Is Lima the capital of Peru? **B: I don't know.** **A:** Is she a good athlete? **B: Yes, I think so.** **A:** Is it hot today? **B: No, I don't think so.**

FOCUSED PRACTICE

❶ DISCOVER THE GRAMMAR

Look at the picture. Then match the questions and answers.

_____ **1.** Is it September 1st?   **a.** No, they aren't.

_____ **2.** Is it 9 o'clock?   **b.** No, she isn't.

_____ **3.** Is Al Brown in class?   **c.** No, it isn't.

_____ **4.** Is Yoko Mori late?   **d.** Yes, he is.

_____ **5.** Are the students worried?   **e.** Yes, it is.

❷ PEOPLE AND PLACES   Grammar Notes 1–3

Write **yes / no** *questions. Then write short and long answers to the questions.*
Use contractions when possible.

1. Al Brown / from New York

    A: ___Is Al Brown from New York?_____

    B: ___No, he's not. (No, he isn't.)_____
       OR

    B: ___No, he's not from New York. He's from Michigan._____

2. you / from Australia

    A: _____

    B: _____
       OR

    B: _____

3. Rio de Janeiro / in Colombia

   A: _____

   B: _____

   OR

   B: _____

4. Canada / near India

   A: _____

   B: _____

   OR

   B: _____

5. Caracas and Mexico City / capital cities

   A: _____

   B: _____

   OR

   B: _____

❸ A DETECTIVE AT WORK   Grammar Notes 1–2

Listen and complete the sentences.

4 THE MYSTERY ENDS   Grammar Note 2

Milt and Pete are talking on the telephone. Listen and read their conversation.

MILT: Hello.

PETE: Hi. Is that you, Milt?

MILT: Yes.

PETE: This is Pete.

MILT: Pete, it's 5 A.M. here.

PETE: Oh, I'm sorry. Any news about Rocky?

MILT: No.

PETE: Carol says, "Rocky is big and strong. With Rocky here, I'm safe. I love him."

MILT: Let me think. She says, "He's big and strong." She's safe with Rocky. Wait a second. I've got it.

PETE: You do?

MILT: Yes. Rocky *is* big and strong. And he lives with Carol and Yoko. I know him.

PETE: What?

MILT: Relax, Pete. Rocky is a dog. Rocky is Yoko's dog.

PETE: Rocky's a dog! Oh, Milt. You *are* a great detective. And I worry too much. Please Milt, don't tell Carol. This is our secret.

Now answer the questions. Use short answers.

1. Is it 5 A.M. in New York? ___No, it's not. (No, it isn't.)___

2. Is it 5 A.M. in Oregon? _____

3. Is Rocky big and strong? _____

4. Is Rocky a man? _____

5. Is Pete worried now? _____

6. Are you surprised? _____

COMMUNICATION PRACTICE

5 FIND SOMEONE WHO'S . . .

hungry

right-handed

a good soccer player

thirsty

from an island

left-handed

Go around the class. Use the words and phrases below to ask classmates **yes / no** *questions. Tell the class some interesting facts about your classmates.*

a good singer	hungry	from a new city
a good dancer	thirsty	from a capital city
a good writer	homesick	from an island
a good artist	right-handed	from an old city
a good soccer player	left-handed	usually early / late

EXAMPLE:
A: Mohammed, are you a good writer?
B: Yes, I am.

6 CARS

Work in small groups. Match the cars and countries.

_____ 1. Fiats and Ferraris are from
_____ 2. Jeeps are from
_____ 3. Hyundais are from
_____ 4. Renaults and Peugeots are from
_____ 5. Toyotas and Nissans are from
_____ 6. Volvos and Saabs are from

a. Sweden
b. France
c. Japan
d. Korea
e. the United States
f. Italy

Now play a game. A student in one group asks a student in another group a
yes / no *question about the cars above or other cars. If the answer is correct,*
the student who answers wins a point for his or her group. The first group with
10 points wins.

EXAMPLE:
GROUP A STUDENT: Are Hyundais from Korea?
GROUP B STUDENT: Yes, they are.
GROUP A STUDENT: You're right. (Group B wins a point)

7 EXPRESSING OPINIONS

Work with a partner. Ask each other **yes / no** *questions. Answer* **Yes, I think so,**
No, I don't think so, *or* **I don't know.** *Check (✔) your partner's answers.*

	Yes, I think so.	No, I don't think so.	I don't know.
1. Is Leonardo DiCaprio a good actor?	☐	☐	☐
2. Is Arnold Schwarzenegger a good actor?	☐	☐	☐
3. Is Celine Dion a good singer?	☐	☐	☐
4. Are Volvos good cars?	☐	☐	☐
5. Are Volvos popular cars?	☐	☐	☐
6. Are Jeeps expensive?	☐	☐	☐
7. Are Jeeps popular?	☐	☐	☐
8. (your own idea)	☐	☐	☐

THE **PAST TENSE** OF **BE;** PAST TIME MARKERS

GRAMMAR **IN CONTEXT**

WARM UP   Are thank you notes easy for you to write?

 Listen and read the thank you note from Pete Winston to Milt Costa.

Dear Milt,

   Thanks for your help **last week.** You **were** wonderful. I **was** very worried about Carol. I know she's 20 and she's an adult, but for me she's still a little girl.

   Regards to your sister.

                          Fondly,
                          Pete

P.S. You're right, Milt. You really are Milt, the Great Detective!

Peter Winston
345 West 76 Street
New York, New York 10024

          Mr. Milt Costa
          2 Maple Street
          Corvallis, Oregon 97333

27

GRAMMAR **PRESENTATION**
THE PAST TENSE OF *BE*; PAST TIME MARKERS

AFFIRMATIVE STATEMENTS

SINGULAR			
SUBJECT	**BE**		**TIME MARKER**
I	**was**		
You	**were**	at a restaurant	**last night.**
He She It	**was**		

PLURAL			
SUBJECT	**BE**		**TIME MARKER**
We You They	**were**	at a restaurant	**last night.**

NEGATIVE STATEMENTS

SINGULAR			
SUBJECT	**BE / NOT**		**TIME MARKER**
I	**was not wasn't**		
You	**were not weren't**	at home	**last night.**
He She It	**was not wasn't**		

PLURAL			
SUBJECT	**BE / NOT**		**TIME MARKER**
We You They	**were not weren't**	at home	**last night.**

YES / NO QUESTIONS

SINGULAR			
BE	**SUBJECT**		**TIME MARKER**
Was	I		
Were	you	at work	**two weeks ago?**
Was	he she it		

PLURAL			
BE	**SUBJECT**		**TIME MARKER**
Were	we you they	at work	**two weeks ago?**

NOTES	EXAMPLES
1. The **past tense** of *be* has two forms: *was* and *were*.	• Bekir **was** late. • They **were** worried.
2. In informal writing and in speaking, use the contractions *wasn't* and *weren't* in negative statements and short answers.	• I **wasn't** in London. • They **weren't** students. • Were they at work? No, they **weren't**.
3. **Past time markers** can go at the beginning or the end of a sentence.	• **Yesterday** he was absent. • He was in Taipei **last week**.

PAST TIME MARKERS

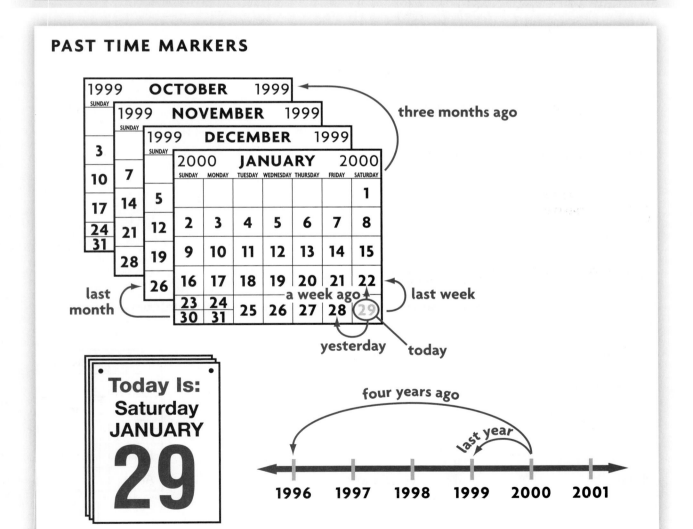

FOCUSED PRACTICE

1 DISCOVER THE GRAMMAR

Read the cartoon. Then circle the correct answer.

How's your teacher?

I don't know. Yesterday 2+2 was 4. Today 3+1 is 4!

1. Was the teacher right yesterday?
   a. Yes, she was.   **b.** No, she wasn't.

2. Is the teacher right today?
   a. Yes, she is.   **b.** No, she isn't.

3. Is the story funny?
   a. Yes, I think so.   **b.** No, I don't think so.

2 CLASS ATTENDANCE   Grammar Notes 1–2

Look at yesterday's attendance sheet (✔ = here). Complete the sentences with **was**, **wasn't**, **were** *and* **weren't**.

	Yesterday
Pierre	absent
Juan	✔
Gloria	✔
Emiko	absent
Anna	absent

1. Pierre and Emiko _____*were*_____ absent yesterday.

   Yesterday they _____ here.

2. Juan and Gloria _____ here yesterday.

3. Anna _____ absent yesterday.

4. Gloria _____ absent yesterday.

What about you?

I _____ yesterday.

❸ AL BROWN'S CLASS

*Al Brown is taking attendance. Listen. Then listen again and write a check (✔), **absent**, or **late** next to the names.*

	Yesterday	**Today**
Yoko Mori	*absent*	✔
Bekir Ada		
Eun Young Kim		
Hector Gonzales		

❹ THE WEATHER

Look at the chart and learn the words for different kinds of weather. Then complete the sentences about the weather in different places.

hot		warm		cool		cold	
sunny		windy		rainy		cloudy	

🌐 World Weather

	LAST WEEK	**ONE MONTH AGO**
Alaska	cold / cloudy	cold / sunny
Bangkok	hot / sunny	hot / sunny
Bogotá	warm / sunny	warm / cloudy

1. A: How was the weather in Bangkok last week?

   B: It ___was___ ___hot___ and ___sunny___.

   A: And one month ago?

   B: One month ago it _____ _____ and _____, too.

2. A: _____ it warm in Alaska last week?

   B: No, it _____.

3. A: Was it sunny in Bogotá last week?

   B: _____, _____ _____.

   A: How was the weather in Bogotá one month ago?

   B: It _____ _____ and _____.

4. A: Was it warm and sunny in Bogotá _____ _____?

   B: Yes, it _____.

COMMUNICATION PRACTICE

5 INFORMATION GAP: THE WEATHER IN CAPITAL CITIES

Work in pairs.

Student A, look at this page. Ask your partner questions to complete the chart.

Student B, look at the Information Gap on page 37 and follow the instructions there.

	Yesterday		Today	
Mexico City	cool / cloudy		cool / cloudy	
São Paulo	warm / sunny		warm / sunny	
Washington, D.C.	cool / cloudy		cool / rainy	
Tokyo	_____		_____	
Seoul	_____		_____	
Taiwan	_____		_____	

World Weather

EXAMPLES:

1. Is it hot in Tokyo today?
2. Was it hot in Tokyo yesterday?
3. How's the weather in Seoul today?
4. How was the weather in Seoul yesterday?

6 GAME

Work with a partner. Write three true and three false sentences. Use the words in the box.

hot	warm	cloudy	rainy	late	absent
cold	cool	sunny	windy	early	here

Now read your sentences to a partner. Your partner says **That's right** *or* **That's wrong** *and corrects the false sentences.*

EXAMPLES:

A: It's hot today.
B: That's right.

A: Juan was late yesterday.
B: That's wrong. Juan was early.

REVIEW OR SELFTEST

I. *Read each conversation. Circle the letter of the underlined word or group of words that is not correct.*

1. **YOKO:** Are you <u>a</u> new student?   **A B C D**
                  A

    BEKIR: Yes, <u>I'm</u>. I'm from Turkey. Where <u>are you</u>
                     B   C
    from?

    YOKO: <u>I'm</u> from Japan.
                 D

2. **JUAN:** You're old <u>student</u>.   **A B C D**
                            A

    YOKO: No, you're wrong. We <u>aren't</u> old students.
                                       B

    Bekir and I <u>are</u> <u>new</u> students.
                    C   D

3. **CAROL:** <u>It's</u> hot here.   **A B C D**
                 A

    YOKO: No, <u>it's not</u>. It's sixty degrees. <u>It's cold</u>.
                     B   C

    CAROL: Well, <u>I hot</u>.
                        D

4. **JUAN:** <u>Was</u> it hot in your room <u>last night</u>?   **A B C D**
                A   B

    YOKO: No, it <u>isn't</u>. <u>It was</u> cold.
                        C   D

5. **JUAN:** <u>Was</u> Yoko and Bekir in class <u>yesterday</u>?   **A B C D**
                A   B

    MARIA: <u>I don't know</u>. I <u>was</u> absent.
                   C   D

II. *Circle the answer that best completes each sentence.*

1. Last week we _____ in Paris.   **A B C D**
   (A) was   (C) is
   (B) are   (D) were

2. Yoko and Carol _____ absent yesterday.   **A B C D**
   (A) were   (C) are
   (B) was   (D) is

3. _____ a detective?   **A B C D**
   (A) Is you   (C) Are you
   (B) You   (D) You are

(continued on next page)

4. John _____ the United States.   **A   B   C   D**
   (A) is from   (C) are from
   (B) am from   (D) were from

5. Are you tired? Yes, _____ .   **A   B   C   D**
   (A) we tired   (C) we be
   (B) we're   (D) we are

6. _____ Carol and Yoko at home last night?   **A   B   C   D**
   (A) Was   (C) Are
   (B) Were   (D) Be

III. Write **yes / no** *questions. Use the words in parentheses.*

A: (cloudy / yesterday) _____

B: No, it wasn't. It was sunny.

A: (cloudy / now) _____

B: Yes.

A: (you / in school / last week) _____

B: Yes, I was.

IV. *Correct this e-mail from Carol to her father. There are three mistakes.*

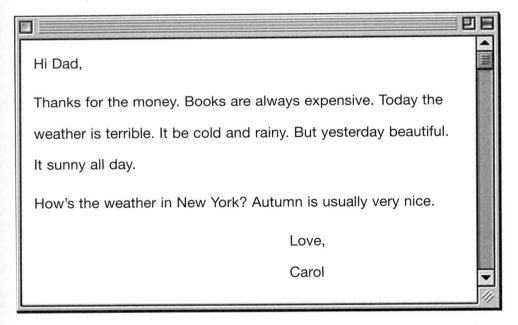

Hi Dad,

Thanks for the money. Books are always expensive. Today the weather is terrible. It be cold and rainy. But yesterday beautiful. It sunny all day.

How's the weather in New York? Autumn is usually very nice.

Love,

Carol

▶ *To check your answers, go to the Answer Key on page 37.*

FROM GRAMMAR TO WRITING CAPITALIZATION

 Look at A and B. What's wrong with A?

A	B
mr. john smith 342 dryden road ithaca, new york 14850	Mr. John Smith 342 Dryden Road Ithaca, New York 14850

Study the information about capitalization.

Capitalization

1. Use a **capital letter** for the first word in every sentence.	• **We** are new students.
2. Use capital letters for **titles**.	• This is **Mr.** Winston. • She is **Dr.** Jones.
3. Use capital letters for the names of **people** and **places** (proper nouns).	• **Lulu Winston** is from **Vancouver, Canada**.
4. Use capital letters for the names of **streets**, **cities**, **states**, **countries**, and **continents**.	• 5 **Elm Street** **West Redding, Connecticut** **U.S.A.**
5. Use a capital letter for the word *I*.	• **I** am happy to be here.

2 *Add capital letters.*

1. this is ms. herrera.

2. her address is 4 riverdale avenue.

3. i'm her good friend.

4. she was in bangkok and taiwan last year.

3 *Correct the postcard from Ellen to Ruth. Add capital letters.*

 Paradise Hotel

Hi ruth,

john and i are in acapulco this week. it's beautiful here. the people are friendly and the weather is great. it's sunny and warm.

last week we were in mexico city for two days. i was there on business. my meetings were long and difficult, but our evenings were fun.

hope all is well with you.

Regards,

ellen

 USA 22

To:

ms. ruth holland

10 oldwick court

ringwood, new jersey 07456

u.s.a.

Write a postcard to a friend.

To:

REVIEW OR SELFTEST
ANSWER KEY

I.
1. B
2. A
3. D
4. C
5. A

II.
1. D
2. A
3. C
4. A
5. D
6. B

III.
1. Was it cloudy yesterday?
2. Is it cloudy now?
3. Were you in school last week?

IV. It *is* cold and rainy. But yesterday *was* beautiful. It *was* sunny all day.

INFORMATION GAP FOR STUDENT B   Unit 4, Exercise 5

Student B, answer your partner's questions. Then ask your partner questions to complete the chart.

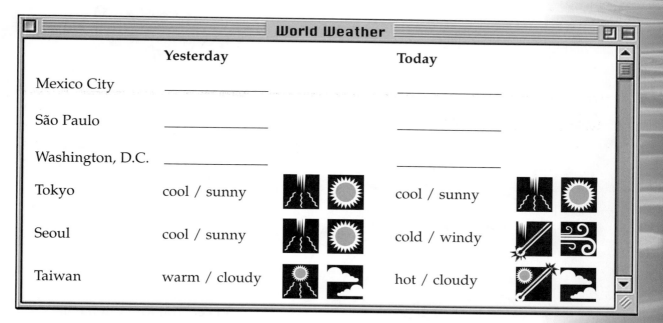

World Weather		
	Yesterday	**Today**
Mexico City	_____	_____
São Paulo	_____	_____
Washington, D.C.	_____	_____
Tokyo	cool / sunny	cool / sunny
Seoul	cool / sunny	cold / windy
Taiwan	warm / cloudy	hot / cloudy

EXAMPLES:
1. Is it hot in Mexico City today?
2. Was it hot in Mexico City yesterday?
3. How's the weather in São Paulo today?
4. How was the weather in São Paulo yesterday?

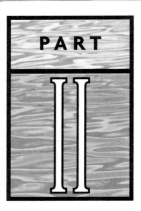

PART II
NOUNS, ADJECTIVES, AND PREPOSITIONS; THE PRESENT PROGRESSIVE

PREVIEW

Lulu Winston and Bertha Bean are friends. Lulu is looking at pictures of her family. Listen and read the conversation.

WONDERFUL SONS, LUCKY DAUGHTERS-IN-LAW

LULU: Come, look at my pictures.

BERTHA: Not more pictures!

LULU: But these are special. They're my favorite pictures.

BERTHA: Okay, okay. Show me your pictures.

LULU: This is Bob at five.

> Come, look at my pictures.

> Not more pictures!

BERTHA: He's cute. What's he doing?

LULU: He's fixing the toilet.

BERTHA: Oh?

LULU: You know, today he's a plumber. He's a very *successful* plumber.

38

BERTHA: I know. I know. Is this Pete?

LULU: Yes. He was eight years old in this photo.

BERTHA: Is he selling drinks?

LULU: Uh-huh. He's selling lemonade and orange juice. Today he's buying and selling businesses.

BERTHA: Are these your grandchildren?

LULU: Yes. They're my wonderful grandchildren.

BERTHA: Who are the women behind your grandchildren?

LULU: They're my daughters-in-law. My sons are so handsome!

BERTHA: They're pretty.

LULU: Pretty? My sons aren't pretty. They're handsome.

BERTHA: Your daughters-in-law are pretty.

LULU: My daughters-in-law are *lucky*. They're married to my wonderful sons.

BERTHA: They're not so lucky. You're their mother-in-law.

COMPREHENSION CHECK

Check (✔) **That's right**, **That's wrong**, *or* **I don't know**.

	That's right.	That's wrong.	I don't know.
1. Lulu thinks her sons are wonderful.	❏	❏	❏
2. Lulu thinks her grandchildren are wonderful.	❏	❏	❏
3. Lulu thinks her daughters-in-law are wonderful.	❏	❏	❏
4. Bertha thinks Lulu's daughters-in-law are lucky.	❏	❏	❏
5. Lulu thinks Bertha's lucky.	❏	❏	❏

WITH A PARTNER

Practice the conversation on pages 38 and 39.

5 COUNT NOUNS; *A / AN*

GRAMMAR **IN CONTEXT**

WARM UP Do you like to take pictures of your family and friends?

Lulu is showing her friend Adele photos of her granddaughters. Listen and read the conversation.

ADELE: Who are they?

LULU: They're my **granddaughters**.

ADELE: Your **granddaughters**? They're lovely. Are they married?

LULU: No, they're single. This is **Norma** on the right. She's **a** Spanish **teacher**. And **Carol**'s on the left. She's **a student**.

ADELE: My **grandson** is **a chef** and **an athlete**. He's single too, and he's new here. Do you think they'd like to meet **a chef**?

LULU: Of course. Everyone loves to eat. But they're not here. **Carol**'s in **Oregon** and **Norma**'s in **Massachusetts**.

ADELE: Invite them here this **winter**. Everyone loves **Florida** in **winter**. I'll introduce them to him.

GRAMMAR **PRESENTATION**
COUNT NOUNS; A / AN

SINGULAR NOUNS (ONE)	PLURAL NOUNS (MORE THAN ONE)

He is **a plumber**.

She is **an artist**.

Florida is **a state**.

They are **plumbers**.

They are **artists**.

Oregon and Florida are **states**.

NOTES

EXAMPLES

1. Nouns are the names of people, places, and things. Use **a** before singular **count nouns** that begin with a consonant sound.

▶ **BE CAREFUL!** Use **a** before a *u* that is pronounced like *u* in *university*.

- She's **a s**tudent.
- He's **a b**usinessman.
- It's **a h**ouse.

- It's **a u**niversity.

(continued on next page)

2. Use *an* before singular count nouns that begin with a vowel sound.

- She's **an a**ctress.
- He's **an e**ngineer.
- It's **an i**ce-cream cone.
- It's **an o**ven.
- It's **an u**mbrella.

▶ **BE CAREFUL!** Use *an* before an *h* that is silent.

- It's **an h**our too early.

3. Do not put *a* or *an* before plural nouns.

- **Lemons** are yellow.

4. The names of people and places are **proper nouns**. These are always capitalized. Do not put *a* or *an* before proper nouns.

- **Bangkok** is the capital of **Thailand**.
- **Lulu** is a grandmother.

5. Do not use *a* or *an* before non-count nouns.

- His **hair** is brown.

REFERENCE NOTE
See Unit 33 for a discussion of non-count nouns.
See Appendix 7, pages A-7 and A-8, for the spelling rules for plural nouns.
See Unit 33 and Appendix 10, page A-10, for the use of the definite article *the*.
See Appendix 18, page A-18, for pronunciation of the phonetic alphabet.

FOCUSED PRACTICE

1 DISCOVER THE GRAMMAR

Read about James Belmont.

James Belmont is a photographer and an artist. He takes photos from all over the world. James is now in Miami. He's a photography teacher at a local college.

Look at the reading again and find the following.

1. Find a noun that begins with a vowel sound. _____

2. Find a proper noun. _____

3. Find a plural noun. _____

2 PEOPLE, PLACES, THINGS

Listen and complete the sentences. Use **a** *or* **an** *before a singular noun. Leave a blank before a plural noun.*

1. He's ___a___ plumber.

2. We are _____ students.

3. It's _____ house.

4. These are _____ watches.

5. It's _____ hour.

6. They are _____ businessmen.

7. We're _____ teachers.

8. These are _____ earrings.

9. She's _____ actress.

10. This is _____ orange.

3 PLURAL NOUNS

Look at the spelling rules for plural nouns on pages A-7 and A-8 in Appendix 7.
Complete the sentences. Use the plural form of each noun.

1. (son) These are my _____sons_____ .

2. (woman) They are _____women_____ .

3. (country) We're from different _____ .

4. (city) Our _____ are far from here.

5. (picture) They are new _____ .

6. (brother) My _____ are tall.

7. (class) My _____ are in room 302 and room 410.

8. (watch) Our _____ are from Japan.

9. (potato) These _____ are big.

10. (dictionary) These _____ are good.

4 EDITING

Yoko and Marcos are in their English class. Read their conversation. Add **a**
or **an** *in two places. Then listen and check your work.*

MARCOS: What's this?

YOKO: It's ⌃ᵃ pen.

MARCOS: Is that eraser?

YOKO: Yes.

MARCOS: Is he teacher?

YOKO: Yes, he is. He's Al Brown.

COMMUNICATION PRACTICE

5 LEARNING THE NAMES OF CLASSROOM OBJECTS

Work with a partner. Look at the picture on page 44 and learn the names of objects in the classroom. Point to the objects and ask your partner questions.

EXAMPLES:

A: Is that a pen?   **A:** What's that?
B: Yes, it's a pen.   **B:** It's a book bag.

Classroom Objects

a desk	an audio cassette recorder	a CD player	a wastepaper basket
a book		a CD (compact disc)	
a notebook	a VCR (video cassette recorder)	a chalkboard	a pen
a book bag		a map	an eraser
a table	a video cassette	a ruler	a computer
			a television

Now make a list of singular and plural objects in your classroom.

Singular	Plural
a VCR	pens

6 MY FAVORITE MONTH, DAY, CITY

Work with a partner. Add words to each list. Tell your partner about your favorites.

EXAMPLES:

My favorite day is Friday.
My favorite month is December.

Days of the Week	Months of the Year	Cities
Sunday	January	Venice
Monday	February	Kyoto

Now tell the class about your partner's favorites.

EXAMPLES:

Maria's favorite day is Friday.
Her favorite month is December.

DESCRIPTIVE ADJECTIVES

GRAMMAR **IN CONTEXT**

WARM UP   Circle the words that describe your home.

big - small	new - old	comfortable - uncomfortable
messy - neat	clean - dirty	safe - dangerous

Listen and read the letter from Carol to Lulu.

Dear Grandma Lulu,

Thanks so much for the cookies. They're **delicious**. I'm **happy** here at Oregon State. My roommate, Yoko, is from Japan. She's a **new** student, too. She's **nice** and very **neat**. She looks like an actress. She's **tall** and **thin**. Her hair is **short** and **straight**.

We have a **small** apartment and a **big** dog. Our dog's name is Rocky. He's **loud** and **lovable**. We're **safe** with Rocky around.

My classes are **interesting**, and my teachers are **friendly**. I'm **lucky** to be here. I hope you're **fine**. Please write.

Love,
Carol

GRAMMAR **PRESENTATION**
DESCRIPTIVE ADJECTIVES

NOUN	BE	ADJECTIVE
Arnold Schwarzenegger	is	**strong**.
Arnold Schwarzenegger and Sylvester Stallone	are	

	ADJECTIVE	NOUN
He is a	**famous**	actor.
They are		actors.

NOTES

EXAMPLES

1. Adjectives describe nouns.

- Arnold Schwarzenegger is **strong**.

2. Adjectives can come after the verb *be*. Adjectives come before a noun.

- Yoko is **young**.
- He is a **famous** man.
  NOT ~~He is a man famous.~~

3. Adjectives do not change form.

singular
- **new** student, **tall** boy

plural
- **new** students, **tall** boys
  NOT ~~news students, talls boys~~

4. When a noun follows an adjective, use **an** before the adjective if the adjective begins with a vowel sound.

- He's **an** interesting actor.

Use **a** before the adjective if the adjective begins with a consonant sound.

- She's **a** strong athlete.

5. Do not use **a** or **an** when the adjective is not followed by a noun.

- It is important.
- He is tall.

FOCUSED PRACTICE

① DISCOVER THE GRAMMAR

Underline the adjective or adjectives in each sentence.

1. The movie was <u>interesting</u>, but it was long.
2. The tall man is a carpenter.
3. That pie was delicious.
4. They are wonderful actors.

② OPPOSITES   Grammar Note 1

Read Carol's letter to her grandmother again. Find an adjective in the letter that means the opposite of each adjective below.

1. big _____small_____
2. boring _____
3. curly _____
4. heavy _____
5. old _____
6. quiet _____
7. long _____
8. unfriendly _____
9. unhappy _____
10. unlucky _____

Dear Grandma Lulu,

Thanks so much for the cookies. They're **delicious**. I'm **happy** here at Oregon State. My roommate, Yoko, is from Japan. She's a **new** student, too. She's **nice** and very **neat**. She looks like an actress. She's **tall** and **thin**. Her hair is **short** and **straight**.

We have a **small** apartment and a **big** dog. Our dog's name is Rocky. He's **loud** and **lovable**. We're **safe** with Rocky around.

My classes are **interesting**, and my teachers are **friendly**. I'm **lucky** to be here. I hope you're **fine**. Please write.

Love,
Carol

③ CLASSROOM OBJECTS   Grammar Notes 1–2

Write questions to complete the conversations. Use the words in slashes.

1. Was / new / it / a / notebook

   A: _Was it a new notebook_____?

   B: Yes, it was.

2. new / Is / tape / the / long

A: _____ ?

B: Yes, it's three hours long.

3. interesting / Are / the / videos

A: _____ ?

B: Yes, they're very interesting.

4 EDITING Grammar Notes 1–4

Correct the mistakes in the conversations.

1. A: Are those ~~olds~~ old videos?

B: Yes, they are. They're from 1985.

A: Are they interestings?

B: I think so.

2. A: That's a computer expensive. Is it new?

B: Yes, it is.

A: Are you happy with it?

B: Yes, it's a good.

3. A: Those news books were longs.

B: Were they interestings?

A: I don't think so.

4. A: Athens is a city old.

B: It's a place interesting.

A: You're right.

COMMUNICATION PRACTICE

5 OUR CITY

Work with a partner. Write adjectives to describe your city.

EXAMPLE:
Our city is clean.

Our city is _____.

6 OBJECTS IN OUR CLASSROOM

Work with a partner. Look around the classroom. Describe objects in your classroom. Use the adjectives in the box.

big	brown	dark	interesting	long	new	small	straight

EXAMPLE:
That's a new notebook.

7 FRIENDS

Work in small groups. Study the adjectives. Use your dictionary for new words. Then check (✓) the words that describe good qualities.

_____ **1.** honest   _____ **5.** cold   _____ **9.** good-looking   _____ **13.** helpful

_____ **2.** friendly   _____ **6.** forgetful   _____ **10.** understanding   _____ **14.** quiet

_____ **3.** warm   _____ **7.** funny   _____ **11.** serious   _____ **15.** shy

_____ **4.** dishonest   _____ **8.** loyal   _____ **12.** kind   _____ **16.** talkative

EXAMPLE:
It's good to be honest.

Now tell about a friend.

EXAMPLE:
A: My friend Janet is very funny. I love to be with her.
B: My friend Sue is not funny, but she's very helpful and kind. That's important to me.

PREPOSITIONS OF PLACE

GRAMMAR **IN CONTEXT**

WARM UP   Look at the picture. Where is Pete?

 🔊 *Listen and read the conversation.*

DR. GRUEN: Hi, Pete.

PETE WINSTON: Hello, George. It's nice to see you. How's your family?

DR. GRUEN: Everyone's fine. How are you?

PETE: OK, but I think I need new glasses.

DR. GRUEN: Well, Pete, let's see. Look at the chart and answer these questions. Where's the Q?

PETE: It's **next to** the W.

DR. GRUEN: Good. And the W?

PETE: The W is **between** the Q and the Z. And the O is **under** the W.

DR. GRUEN: Wonderful. And what's **under** my nose?

PETE: Your nose? That's easy. A handsome, new mustache.

DR. GRUEN: Your eyesight is excellent. See you here next year.

PETE: Great. And see you at the concert next week.

GRAMMAR **PRESENTATION**
PREPOSITIONS OF PLACE

These are common prepositions of place.

under   **behind** **on** **next to**

between **near**   **in**

The briefcase is **under** the desk.

The blackboard is **behind** the desk.

The dictionary is **on** the desk.

The apple is **on** the desk, too.
It is **next to** the dictionary.

The apple is **between** the
dictionary and the computer.

The computer is **near** the
apple and the dictionary.

The newspaper is **in** the
wastepaper basket.

NOTES

1. Prepositions of place tell where
something is. Some common prepositions
of place are *under, behind, on, next to,
between, near, in*.

▶ **BE CAREFUL!** *Near* and *next to* are not the
same. Look at the letters of the alphabet:

ABCDEFGHIJKLMNOPQRSTUVWXYZ

EXAMPLES

- My book bag is **under** my seat.
- Your umbrella is **near** the door.

- The letter A is **next to** the letter B. It is
near the letter B, too.
- The letter A is **near** the letter C, but it
is not **next to** the letter C.
- The letter J is not **next to** the letter A.
- It is not **near** the letter A, either.

FOCUSED PRACTICE

1 DISCOVER THE GRAMMAR

Look at the pictures. Complete the sentences.

__e__ 1. The teacher is

_____ 2. The briefcase, dictionary, apple, and computer are

_____ 3. The wastepaper basket is

_____ 4. The VCR is

_____ 5. The apple is on the desk. It's

_____ 6. The dictionary is on the desk. It's

_____ 7. The blackboard is

_____ 8. The newspaper is

a. on the desk.

b. under the television.

c. in the wastepaper basket.

d. between the computer and the dictionary.

e. under the desk.

f. behind the desk.

g. near the desk.

h. next to the apple.

2 A COCKROACH IN THE KITCHEN! **Grammar Note 1**

Look at Yoko and Carol's kitchen.

*Put an **R** on the refrigerator.*
*Put an **N** on the napkin.*
*Put an **S** on the sink.*
*Put an **ST** on the stove.*
*Put a **C** on the counter.*

Listen to the conversation. Yoko and Carol are very unhappy. There's a cockroach in their kitchen. Put checks (✔) where the cockroach was. Then complete the sentence.

	A			**B**
1. on the refrigerator	✔	*or*	under the refrigerator	☐
2. on the counter	☐		under the counter	☐
3. on the napkin	☐		under the napkin	☐
4. between the counter and the sink	☐		between the sink and the stove	☐

5. At the end of the conversation, Carol and Yoko are _____.

    a. happy   **b.** unhappy

COMMUNICATION PRACTICE

3 GUESS THE COUNTRY

Work with a partner. Write sentences about a country's location. Use the prepositions **between, near, next to,** *and* **in**. *Read your sentences to your partner. Your partner guesses the country. (See the map on pages A-0 and A-1.)*

EXAMPLE:

This country is between Japan and China. It's near Mongolia. It's next to China. It's in Asia. What country is it?

4 TEST YOUR MEMORY

Work with a partner. Your partner closes his or her eyes. Ask your partner where objects in your classroom are. Then ask your partner where classmates are.

EXAMPLES:

A: Where's the chalkboard?   **A:** Where's Maria?
B: It's near the door.   **B:** She's between Luis and Yuriko.

Now ask your partner about places in your school. Use the words in the box.

cafeteria	water fountain	ladies' room	library
elevator	stairs / staircase	mens' room	

EXAMPLE:

A: Where is the cafeteria?
B: It's next to the library.

5 A WORD GAME

One student reads the following clues to the class. The clues spell a word. The class listens and guesses the word.

Clues:

1. There are seven letters in this word.
2. The first letter is *e*.
3. The last letter is *h*.
4. The letter *n* is next to the *e*. What is the word?
5. The letter *s* is next to the *h*. What is the word?
6. The letter *n* is between the *e* and a *g*. What is the word?
7. The letter *s* is between the *h* and an *i*. What is the word?
8. The letter *l* is in the middle. What is the word?

The word is _____ _____ _____ _____ _____ _____ _____.

Write your own word puzzle. Read it to your class.

PRESENT PROGRESSIVE

GRAMMAR IN CONTEXT

WARM UP   In some countries the jobs of men and women are changing. More women in the United States are becoming police officers, bus drivers, doctors, and lawyers. What's happening in your country?

PERCENTAGE OF WOMEN LAW AND MEDICAL SCHOOL GRADUATES (UNITED STATES)			
Law School		**Medical School**	
1960	2.5%	1960	5.5%
1995	42.6%	1995	38.8%

Elenore is talking to her mother-in-law, Lulu. Listen and read their telephone conversation.

ELENORE: Hello?

LULU: Hi, Elenore. This is Lulu.

ELENORE: Hello, Lulu. How are you doing?

LULU: I'm fine. How are my wonderful grandchildren?

ELENORE: Everyone's okay. You know, **Norma's working** in Boston. **She's teaching.** Doug's the captain of his soccer team.

LULU: That's great. How's Carol?

ELENORE: Well, she's at school. I hope **she's studying.** Carol's not a letter writer, but I'm sure she's fine.

LULU: Is Pete there? **Is he watching** the tennis matches on TV?

ELENORE: No, **he isn't watching** TV. He's not here right now. **He's doing** the laundry.

LULU: *What's* my son doing?

ELENORE: The laundry.

LULU: Oh. My poor baby.

ELENORE: What was that?

LULU: Nothing. What's Doug doing now?

ELENORE: He's at the supermarket. **He's shopping.**

LULU: And what about you? What are you doing?

ELENORE: **I'm doing** the taxes.

LULU: *You're* **doing** the taxes! That's a man's job.

GRAMMAR **PRESENTATION**
PRESENT PROGRESSIVE

AFFIRMATIVE STATEMENTS		
SUBJECT	**BE**	**BASE FORM OF VERB + -ING**
I	**am**	
You	**are**	
He She It	**is**	**working**.
We You They	**are**	

NEGATIVE STATEMENTS			
SUBJECT	**BE**	**NOT**	**BASE FORM OF VERB + -ING**
I	**am**		
You	**are**		
He She It	**is**	**not**	**working**.
We You They	**are**		

YES / NO QUESTIONS		
BE	**SUBJECT**	**BASE FORM OF VERB + -ING**
Am	I	
Are	you	
Is	he she it	**working** today?
Are	we you they	

SHORT ANSWERS						
AFFIRMATIVE				**NEGATIVE**		
Yes,	you	**are**.	No,	you**'re**		not.
	I	**am**.		I**'m**		
	he she it	**is**.		he**'s** she**'s** it**'s**		
	you we they	**are**.		you**'re** we**'re** they**'re**		

NOTES

1. Use the **present progressive** (also called the *present continuous*) to talk about an action that is happening now (as you are speaking).

Past ◄─────X─────► Future
Now

EXAMPLES

- The baby **is crying**. She's hungry.
- **It's raining** today.

2. Do not repeat the subject and the verb *be* when the subject is doing two things.

- Doug is **eating** and **drinking**. NOT ~~Doug is eating and Doug is drinking.~~

3. The subject and *be* are reversed when asking a *yes / no* question in the present progressive.

statement
- **He is** working.

question
- **Is he** working?

4. Use **contractions** in speaking and in informal writing.

- **I'm** not cooking. **I'm** doing the laundry.
- Elenore **isn't** cleaning. **She's** doing the taxes.
- We **aren't** working. **We're** resting.

5. Use contractions in negative answers in speaking and writing.

- No, **you're not**. OR No, **you aren't**.

6. We usually use short answers in speaking, but we can also use long answers.

- Is she sleeping?
- **No.** OR **No, she's not sleeping.**
- **No, she's not.** OR **No, she's not sleeping.**
- **No, she isn't.** OR **No, she isn't sleeping.**

REFERENCE NOTE
See Appendix 13, page A-13, for spelling rules for the present progressive.
See Unit 26 for verbs that are not usually used in the progressive form.

FOCUSED PRACTICE

1 DISCOVER THE GRAMMAR

Listen and read the weather and traffic report. Underline the present progressive. Then answer the questions.

> Good morning. This is Ted Treitel with this morning's weather and traffic. Take your umbrellas. It's raining right now in midtown, and the temperature is 40 degrees Fahrenheit. As for traffic, Route 5 is a good road into the city. Cars are moving quickly. But don't take Highway 11. There's an accident, and cars aren't moving at all.

Check (✔) True or False.

	True	False
1. It's raining in midtown.	❏	❏
2. Cars aren't moving on Route 5.	❏	❏
3. Cars aren't moving on Highway 11.	❏	❏

2 FAMILY PICTURES   Grammar Notes 1, 3–4

Complete the conversation. Use the present progressive and the verb in parentheses.

BERTHA: That's a wonderful picture of Carol.

_____Is_____ she ____wearing____ a costume?
                                 1. (wear)

LULU: No. That's not a costume. She _____ a
                                              2. (wear)

cape. It was a present from me. Look.

Here's Doug.

BERTHA: He's very serious.

LULU: I know. He _____ because
                        3. (smile, not)

he's worried about soccer. Soccer is his

life this year.

BERTHA: _____ Elenore and Pete _____

4. (have)

a fight?

LULU: I don't think so. I think they _____.

5. (dance)

It's a strange picture of them.

BERTHA: Okay, Lulu. Enough pictures. Let's go out for lunch.

It's 12:00. They _____ a lunch special at

6. (offer)

China Palace between 11:30 and 12:30.

LULU: Okay. I _____ hungry.

7. (get)

3 WHAT ARE THEY DOING?

Grammar Notes 4–6

Write **yes / no** *questions in the present progressive. Then read the conversation on page 55 again and answer the questions. Use short answers.*

1. Lulu / talk to Pete

A: Is Lulu talking to Pete?

B: No she's not. (No, she isn't.)

2. Doug / shop

A: _____

B: _____

3. Elenore / do laundry

A: _____

B: _____

4. Lulu and Elenore / talk about the weather

A: _____

B: _____

5. Pete / watch TV

A: _____

B: _____

4 A DUANE HANSON SCULPTURE

Duane Hanson is an American artist. His sculptures show Americans doing everyday things. This is a photo of one of his sculptures. Write about it. Use the present progressive in your sentences.

1. sit / at a table

   Two people __are sitting at a table.__

2. wear jeans, a plaid shirt, leather shoes

   The _____

3. a house dress

   The _____

4. watches

   Both of them _____

5. wear glasses

   The _____

6. read / eat ice cream

   _____

7. look at / the woman

   The _____

8. not talk

   They _____

COMMUNICATION PRACTICE

5 WHAT AM I DOING NOW?

Check the sentences that are true for you.

1. ☑ I'm holding a pen. ☐ I'm not holding a pen.
2. ☐ I'm sitting next to a man. ☐ I'm not sitting next to a man.
3. ☐ I'm sitting next to a woman with glasses. ☐ I'm not sitting next to a woman with glasses.
4. ☐ I'm looking out the window. ☐ I'm not looking out the window.
5. ☐ I'm wearing comfortable shoes. ☐ I'm not wearing comfortable shoes.
6. ☐ I'm wearing a watch. ☐ I'm not wearing a watch.
7. ☐ I'm wearing jeans. ☐ I'm not wearing jeans.
8. ☐ I'm thinking about the present progressive. ☐ I'm not thinking about the present progressive.
9. ☐ I'm daydreaming. ☐ I'm not daydreaming.
10. ☐ I'm smiling. ☐ I'm not smiling.
11. ☐ I'm _____ (your own idea) ☐ I'm not _____.

Read your sentences to a partner. Listen to his or her sentences. What are both you and your partner doing now? Tell the class.

EXAMPLES:
We are both wearing comfortable shoes.
We are not holding pens.

6 CAN I CALL YOU BACK LATER?

Work with a partner. Practice the telephone conversation. Use the verbs in the box and your own ideas. Partner A calls Partner B. Partner B is busy and wants to call Partner A back later. Then Partner B calls, but Partner A wants to call back later.

study	write a letter	read my e-mail	watch TV and eat
work	eat	take a bath / shower	clean
your own idea			

EXAMPLE:
ALI: Hello, Juan. This is Ali.
JUAN: Hi, Ali.
ALI: Are you busy, Juan?
JUAN: Well, I'm watching a good movie on TV. Can I call you back in a few minutes?
ALI: Sure.

(continued on next page)

Repeat your telephone conversations for the class. Listen to your classmates' conversations. Write down what each student is doing.

EXAMPLES:
Juan is watching a movie on TV.
Emiko is reading her e-mail.

 INFORMATION GAP: WHAT'S THE DIFFERENCE?

Work with a partner.

Partner A, look at this picture. Write sentences about your picture. Use the verbs in the box. Then, talk with your partner about the differences in your pictures. Find five differences.

Partner B, look at the Information Gap on page 67 and follow the instructions.

| chase | eat | fight | play | rain | read | sleep | watch TV |

EXAMPLE:
A: In my picture, the father is watching TV.
B: In my picture, he's . . .
A: Is the mother reading and eating popcorn in your picture?

 CHARADES

Act out a situation in front of your class. The class guesses what you are doing.

Suggestions
You are watching a sad movie.
You are sleeping and snoring.
You are reading a boring book.
You are telling your friend a secret.
You are eating very spicy food.
You are arguing about your bill at a restaurant.
You are sewing.

9 **GAME: WHAT'S EVERYONE WEARING?**

A. *Work with a partner. Look at the illustration. Label the clothes and accessories.*

a. watch	**e.** cap	**i.** overalls	**m.** glasses
b. earring	**f.** sweatshirt	**j.** shoes (athletic)	**n.** blouse
c. ring	**g.** skirt	**k.** socks	**o.** vest
d. belt	**h.** shoes (loafers)	**l.** sweater	**p.** pants/slacks

B. *Partner A, look at your classmates for a minute. Close your eyes. Try to answer your partner's questions. Partner B, ask* **yes / no** *questions about students in the class.*

EXAMPLE:
B: Is Maria wearing a short skirt and small earrings?
A: No, she isn't. She's wearing a long skirt and big earrings.

PART

II

REVIEW OR SELFTEST

I. *Read each conversation. Circle the letter of the underlined word or group of words that is not correct.*

1. **A:** Is <u>it's</u> raining outside?
        A B

   B: Yes, <u>it is</u>. I'm <u>not</u> leaving.
              C   D

   A B C D

2. **A:** <u>Are they</u> <u>play</u> soccer?
            A   B

   B: <u>No</u>, they're <u>playing</u> baseball.
            C   D

   A B C D

3. **A:** <u>She's wearing</u> <u>a</u> red blouse.
            A   B

   B: No, she's <u>no</u> wearing a red blouse. She's wearing a
                      C

   <u>red</u> sweater.
   D

   A: Oh.

   A B C D

4. **A:** <u>Are</u> <u>they</u> <u>youngs</u> men?
            A   B   C

   B: <u>I think so</u>. They're in college.
            D

   A B C D

5. **A:** They're <u>news</u> <u>students</u>.
                    A   B

   B: No, they <u>aren't</u>. They're <u>old</u> students.
                     C   D

   A B C D

II. *Complete the sentences. Circle the correct answers.*

1. He is _____.
   (A) a man strong
   (B) a strong man
   (C) strong man
   (D) strong men

   A B C D

2. They are my _____.
   (A) grandchild
   (B) the grandchildren
   (C) a grandchild
   (D) grandchildren

   A B C D

3. This is _____.
   (A) oranges
   (B) a orange
   (C) an orange
   (D) an oranges

   A B C D

4. Is this _____?
   (A) clean towel
   (B) clean towels
   (C) towels clean
   (D) a clean towel

   A B C D

5. Are _____?
   (A) you sleeping
   (B) you sleep
   (C) sleeping
   (D) you be sleeping

   A B C D

64

III. _Complete the sentences. Use **a** or **an** or leave a blank._

1. He isn't _____ teacher. He's _____ student. He's _____ new in this school.

2. She isn't _____ actress. She's _____ singer.

3. They're _____ famous. They're _____ actors.

4. Our grammar class isn't long. It's _____ hour.

5. This is _____ hospital. It's near the university.

6. He's _____ uncle. She's _____ aunt. This is their nephew.

7. This is _____ grammar book. It's _____ helpful book. It's _____ interesting, too.

IV. _Complete the sentences. Use the words in the box. Look at the world map on pages A-0 and A-1 if you need help._

| between | in | next to |

1. France is _____ Europe.

2. The United States is _____ the Atlantic Ocean and the Pacific Ocean.

3. Pakistan is _____ India.

4. Brazil is _____ South America.

V. _Complete the paragraph. Use the affirmative and negative present progressive of each verb in parentheses._

Carol and her friend Dan are at the library, but they're not studying now.

Carol _____ a letter. Her American history book is on the table, but she
1. (write)

_____ the history book. Carol _____ next to Dan. Dan's biology
2. (read) 3. (sit)

book is in front of him, but he _____ his biology book. He _____
4. (read) 5. (look)

at a magazine. Carol and Dan _____ and _____ a break.
6. (relax) 7. (take)

They _____ now.
8. (work)

▶ _**To check your answers, go to the Answer Key on page 67.**_

FROM GRAMMAR TO WRITING
SUBJECTS AND VERBS

PART II

1 *What's wrong with these sentences?*

A

1. He a handsome man.
2. She a red skirt.
3. I from Argentina.

B

1. Am wearing blue pants.
2. Are tired?
3. Is a cool day.

All sentences in A are missing a verb.

All sentences in B are missing a subject.

Study the information about subjects and verbs.

Subjects and Verbs Every sentence needs a subject and verb.	
The **subject** is a noun or pronoun. It tells who or what did something.	• **John** is running. • **They** are watching TV.
The **verb** tells the action or links the subject with the rest of the sentence.	• It **is raining**. • He **is** a doctor.

2 *Correct this paragraph. Then underline the subject and circle the verb in each sentence.*

I in Central Park. It a sunny day in September. Is crowded. Some children soccer. They're laughing and shouting. Some people are jogging. Three older women on a bench. Are watching the joggers and soccer players. A young man and woman are holding hands. Are smiling. Are in love. Central Park a wonderful place to be on a beautiful September day.

3 *Imagine you are in one of the following places. Write one paragraph about the people you see there.*

1. You are on a bus.
2. You are in a restaurant or cafeteria.
3. You are in a park.

REVIEW OR SelfTest
ANSWER KEY

I.
1. B
2. B
3. C
4. C
5. A

II.
1. B
2. D
3. C
4. D
5. A

III.
1. a; a; _____
2. an; a
3. _____; _____
4. an
5. a
6. an; an
7. a; a; _____

IV.
1. in
2. between
3. next to
4. in

V.
1. is writing
2. isn't reading
3. 's sitting (is sitting)
4. 's not reading (isn't reading)
5. 's looking (is looking)
6. are relaxing
7. taking
8. aren't working

INFORMATION GAP FOR STUDENT B   Unit 8, Exercise 7

Partner B, look at this picture. Write sentences about your picture. Use the verbs in the box. Then, talk with your partner about the differences in your pictures. Find five differences.

| chase | eat | fight | play | rain | read | sleep | watch TV |

EXAMPLE:
A: In my picture, the father is watching TV.
B: In my picture, he's . . .
A: Is the mother reading and eating popcorn in your picture?

PART III

WH- QUESTIONS; POSSESSIVES; PREPOSITIONS OF TIME

PREVIEW

Carol is looking at a photograph of her family. Listen and read the conversation between Yoko and Carol.

THE WINSTON FAMILY

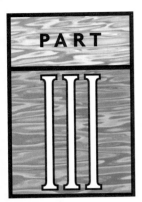

YOKO: What are you looking at?

CAROL: A photo of my family. It was in that package from my Mom.

YOKO: Whose birthday was it?

CAROL: My Dad's. He was fifty.

YOKO: When was that?

CAROL: Last summer.

YOKO: Where were you?

CAROL: In Cape Cod, Massachusetts.

YOKO: Who's standing on the left? Is that your sister?

CAROL: Uh-huh. That's Norma. She lives in Massachusetts. She's a Spanish teacher. We're very different.

YOKO: Oh?

CAROL: She's serious about everything. She wants to save the world. Not like me. She loves animals and she's a vegetarian. I like animals, but I live on chicken and burgers.

YOKO: You *are* different. How old is she?

CAROL: She's twenty-six years old, six years older than me. She's divorced.

YOKO: Who's that?

CAROL: Doug, my younger brother. He's fifteen and in his second year of high school. He lives with my parents. These days Doug and my Dad are having problems.

YOKO: What are they fighting about?

CAROL: About his music, his hair, and his grades.

YOKO: I think he's cute. Who's behind the cake? Is that your Dad?

CAROL: Yes. He's like Norma, very serious. He's a businessman.
My parents and my brother live in New York. My Mom, Elenore, is standing next to Doug.

YOKO: She looks happy.

CAROL: She usually is. She's a writer and a people person. Actually, she gets along well with everyone except my Grandma Lulu.

YOKO: And that's Grandma Lulu.

CAROL: Right. Grandma Lulu lives in Florida. She's seventy-three.

YOKO: Seventy-three? She looks great.

CAROL: I know, but she's lonely. She doesn't work. She lives in Florida and her two sons live far away.

YOKO: How old's your Mom?

CAROL: Forty-nine. And that, of course, is me.

YOKO: It's a great picture of you.

CAROL: Thanks.

COMPREHENSION CHECK

Label the people in the picture. Then complete the chart about the Winstons.

NAME	AGE	OCCUPATION	LIVES IN
Carol			
Norma			
Doug			
Pete			
Elenore			
Lulu			

WITH A PARTNER

Practice the conversation on pages 68 and 69.

QUESTIONS WITH
WHO, WHAT, AND *WHERE*

GRAMMAR **IN CONTEXT**

WARM UP   What's a nice birthday gift for an older person?

Listen and read the conversation between Lulu and her friend Bertha.

LULU: **Who**'s there?

BERTHA: It's me, Bertha.

LULU: Oh, come on in.

BERTHA: Hi. You know, I was here an hour ago and you weren't home. **Where** were you?

LULU: At the hairdresser's.

BERTHA: Oh, I *see.* Your hair is beautiful.

LULU: Thanks. **What**'s that?

BERTHA: It's a small gift.

LULU: A gift? **Who**'s it for?

BERTHA: For you. It's October 15th. Happy birthday.

LULU: Oh, Bertha. Thanks so much. It's heavy. **What** is it? Is it a book?

BERTHA: No, it's a photo album.

LULU: How lovely. Thank you, thank you, thank you. I feel like I'm twenty-one, not seventy-one.

BERTHA: You're not seventy-one. You're seventy-three.

LULU: Shh. It's a secret.

WHAT'S YOUR OPINION?

Is it impolite to ask people their age?

GRAMMAR **PRESENTATION**
QUESTIONS WITH *WHO, WHAT,* AND *WHERE*

QUESTIONS WITH *WHO*

QUESTIONS			ANSWERS
QUESTION WORD	*BE*		
Who	is	Lulu's friend?	Bertha. Bertha is. Bertha is Lulu's friend.
Who	are	friends?	Lulu and Bertha. Lulu and Bertha are. Lulu and Bertha are friends.

QUESTIONS WITH *WHAT*

QUESTIONS			ANSWERS
QUESTION WORD	*BE*		
What	is	lovely?	The photo album. The photo album is. The photo album is lovely.
What	are	these books?	Dictionaries. They're dictionaries. These books are dictionaries.

QUESTIONS WITH *WHERE*

QUESTIONS			ANSWERS
QUESTION WORD	*BE*		
Where	is	Lulu?	At the hairdresser's. She's at the hairdresser's.
Where	are	the presents?	On the table. They're on the table.

NOTES	EXAMPLES
1. *Wh-* **questions** (or information questions) ask for information. They cannot be answered with a *yes* or *no*.	**A:** **What** is it? **B:** It's a book.
2. Use *who* for questions about people.	**A:** **Who**'s seventy-three years old? **B:** Lulu is.
3. Use *what* for questions about things.	**A:** **What**'s a secret? **B:** Lulu's age.
4. Use *where* for questions about locations.	**A:** **Where** was Lulu? **B:** At the hairdresser.
5. We sometimes use contractions for *wh-* questions with *is* in speaking and informal writing.	• **Who's** there? • **What's** his last name? • **Where's** the dictionary?

FOCUSED PRACTICE

1 DISCOVER THE GRAMMAR

Read about Pete's business trip. Then match the questions and answers.

Last week Pete was in Bangkok on business. His flight was long and boring, but his trip was a success.

_____ **1.** Who was in Bangkok last week?

_____ **2.** Where was Pete last week?

_____ **3.** What was long and boring?

a. Pete's flight to Bangkok.

b. In Bangkok.

c. Pete was.

2 CAN YOU DO ME A FAVOR?   Grammar Notes 1–5

Read and learn these phrases. Then listen to the telephone conversation between Elenore and Pete.

at the movies   at the theater   at a ball game   at a party

at a concert   at work   at school   at home

in the kitchen   in the living room   in the bedroom   in the bathroom

(continued on next page)

Now circle the correct answers to the questions.

1. Where's Elenore?

   (**a.** at Doug's school)   **b.** at home   **c.** at a ball game

2. What's in the living room?

   a. a newspaper   **b.** a notebook   **c.** a book

3. Who's at home?

   a. Bertha   **b.** Elenore   **c.** Pete

4. Where's Lulu?

   a. at a concert   **b.** at the movies   **c.** at the theater

5. What's the name of the book Elenore wants?

   a. *The Color Purple*   **b.** *The Red and the Black*   **c.** *The Color of Water*

---

❸ TELEPHONE CALLS   Grammar Notes 1–5

A. *Listen and complete the phone conversations in Part 1. Use* **who's**, **what**, **what's**, *and* **where**.

Part 1

JEFF'S MOTHER: Hello. _____ this?
                      1.

DOUG: Hi, Mrs. Kim. It's Doug. Is Jeff there?

JEFF'S MOTHER: Oh, hi Doug. No, I'm sorry. Jeff isn't here.

DOUG: _____ is he?
           2.

JEFF'S MOTHER: He's at a party.

DOUG: Please tell him I called.

NOAH'S FATHER: Hello?

DOUG: Hi, Mr. Jones. Is Noah there?

NOAH'S FATHER: No, I'm sorry. _____ this?
                         3.

DOUG: It's Doug Winston.

NOAH'S FATHER: Oh, hi Doug. I think Noah's at the movies.

DOUG: Well, please tell him I called.

DINO'S SISTER: Hello.

DOUG: Hello. This is Doug. Is Dino there?

DINO'S SISTER: Oh, hi Doug. Dino isn't here now. He's watching a ball game at Sue's house. *[background noise]*

DOUG: Excuse me. _____ was that?
4.

DINO'S SISTER: He's at Sue's house.

DOUG: Well, please tell him I called.

ELENORE: _____ the matter Doug?
5.

DOUG: Jeff's at a party, Noah's at the movies, and Dino's at Sue's house. Today is my birthday and all my friends are busy.

B. *Answer the questions. Then listen and complete Part 2.*

1. Where's Jeff? _____

2. Who's at the movies? _____

3. What's special about today for Doug? _____

Part 2

[Ten minutes later the doorbell rings, and Doug opens the door.]

NOAH, JEFF, DINO: _____ _____

DOUG: You guys are really something.

COMMUNICATION PRACTICE

4 NOBODY IS HOME

Make up a telephone conversation. Practice the conversation with a partner.

A: Hello.

B: _____. This is _____. Is _____ there?

A: _____.

B: Where is he?

A: _____.

B: Well, what about _____?

A: _____.

B: Please tell them I called.

5 WHERE ARE THEY?

Work with a partner. Read the following sentences. Guess where the people are.
(There are many correct answers.)

1. **LULU:** Hi, Bertha. Please come in.

   Where's Lulu? I think she's at home._____

2. **DOUG:** This music is great.

   Where's Doug? _____

3. **ELENORE:** Shh! Please be quiet. This book is hard to understand.

   Where's Elenore? _____

4. **CAROL:** Ouch! The water's hot.

   Where's Carol? _____

5. **VALERIE:** Oh Pete, Elenore. I'm so glad you're here. Please come in. The drinks are here and the food is over there.

   Where are Pete and Elenore? _____

6 OUR OPINIONS

Complete the questions and answer them for yourself. Then ask a partner the questions and complete the chart with your partner's answers.

You	Your Partner
1. ____What's____ your favorite subject?	
2. _____ two good writers?	
3. _____ your favorite vegetable?	
4. _____ two good new movies?	
5. _____ a good actor?	
6. _____ two beautiful cities?	
7. _____ your favorite sport?	
8. _____ two good TV shows?	

Do you and your partner like the same people and the same things?

7 A MEMORY GAME

One student studies the class and the classroom. Then the student sits in the front of the class with his or her eyes closed. The class asks questions about people and things in the room.

EXAMPLE:
Who's next to the door?
What's between the _____ and the _____?
Where's John?

10 POSSESSIVE NOUNS AND POSSESSIVE ADJECTIVES; QUESTIONS WITH *WHOSE*

GRAMMAR **IN CONTEXT**

WARM UP   Are grades important in a language class? Why?

Al Brown is talking to the students in his class. He has three papers without names. Listen and read the conversation.

AL BROWN: **Whose** composition is this?

BEKIR: Is it a good paper?

AL BROWN: It's excellent.

BEKIR: It's **my** composition.

YOLANDA: No, that's not your handwriting. It's **Yoko's** composition. She's absent today.

AL BROWN: Thanks, Yolanda. **Whose** paper is this?

BEKIR: Is it a good paper?

AL BROWN: It's okay.

BEKIR: I think it's **my** composition.

JUAN: It's not **your** composition. It's **my** composition. See, **my** name is on the back.

AL BROWN: Okay, Juan. Here's **your** composition. **Whose** composition is this?

BEKIR: Is it a good paper?

AL BROWN: Well, it needs work.

BEKIR: It isn't **my** composition.

AL BROWN: Oh yes it is. I have a grade for everyone else.

GRAMMAR **PRESENTATION**
POSSESSIVE NOUNS AND ADJECTIVES; QUESTIONS WITH *WHOSE*

POSSESSIVE NOUNS	
SINGULAR NOUNS	**PLURAL NOUNS**
Lulu's last name is Winston.	The **girls'** gym is on this floor.
That **boy's** book bag is next to mine.	The **boys'** gym is near the elevator.

POSSESSIVE ADJECTIVES		
SUBJECT PRONOUNS	**POSSESSIVE ADJECTIVES**	**EXAMPLE SENTENCES**
I	**my**	**I** am a student. **My** name is Carol.
you	**your**	**You** are next to me. **Your** seat is here.
he	**his**	**He's** a professor. **His** subject is computers.
she	**her**	**She's** my grandmother. **Her** name is Lulu.
it	**its**	**It's** Yoko's dog. **Its** name is Rocky.
we	**our**	**We** are businessmen. **Our** business is in the United States and Asia.
you	**your**	**You** are students. **Your** classroom is near the gym.
they	**their**	**They** are students. **Their** school is in Oregon.

QUESTIONS WITH *WHOSE*	
QUESTIONS	**ANSWERS**
Whose hair is long?	Carol**'s**. Carol**'s** is. Carol**'s** hair is long.
Whose eyes are blue?	Carol**'s**. Carol**'s** are. Carol**'s** eyes are blue.
Whose pen is this?	Yoko**'s**. It's Yoko**'s**. It's Yoko**'s** pen.
Whose pens are these?	Yoko**'s**. They're Yoko**'s**. They're Yoko**'s** pens.

NOTES	EXAMPLES
1. Possessive nouns and **possessive adjectives** show belonging.	• **Elenore's car** (the car belongs to Elenore) • **her** car (the car belongs to her)
2. Add an **apostrophe (')** + **s** to a **singular noun** to show possession. Add an **apostrophe (')** to a **plural noun** ending in *s* to show possession.	• That's Yoko**'s** paper. • The boy**s'** gym is on the third floor.
3. Possessive adjectives replace **possessive nouns**. Possessive adjectives agree with the possessive noun they replace, not the noun that follows.	**His** • ~~Doug's~~ sisters are in Oregon and Massachusetts. **Her** • ~~Carol's~~ brother is in New York.

4. A **noun** always follows a possessive noun or a possessive adjective.
 	
▶ **BE CAREFUL!** Do not confuse "Carol's" in "Carol's hair is long" with "Carol's" in "Carol's a student."
 	
Do not confuse *its* and *it's*.
its = possessive adjective; *it's* = *it is*
	noun
	• **Yoko's book** is new.
	      noun
	• **Her book** is new.
	
	    subject verb
	• **Carol's hair** is long.
	  subject verb
	• **Carol's** a student.
	
	• This is my turtle. **Its** name is Tubby.
	• **It's** a hot day.

5. Use *whose* for questions about possession. ▶ **BE CAREFUL!** *Who's* is the contraction of *who is*. It sounds like the possessive *whose*.	• **Whose** notebook is this? • **Who's** a student? Carol is. • **Whose** hair is long? Carol's is.

REFERENCE NOTE
See Appendix 8, page A-8, for more rules about possessive nouns.

FOCUSED PRACTICE

1 DISCOVER THE GRAMMAR

Read the conversation between Carol and Yoko. Underline the possessive adjectives. Circle the possessive nouns.

CAROL: Hey, Yoko, the apartment looks great, but where are all <u>my</u> things?

YOKO: What are you looking for?

CAROL: Well, for one, where's (Grandma Lulu's) letter?

YOKO: Her letter? It's in the desk drawer.

CAROL: Oh, I see it. Where's Dan's cap? It was on the sofa before.

YOKO: His cap is in the closet.

CAROL: Got it. And what about my brother's and sister's birthday cards?

YOKO: Their cards are on the table over there. Anything else?

CAROL: No, I think that's all.

2 FAMILY RELATIONSHIPS   Grammar Notes 1–2, 4

Complete the sentences. Use the words in the box.

grandmother	mother	aunt	sister	sister-in-law	niece	me
grandfather	father	uncle	brother	brother-in-law	nephew	

1. My mother's mother is my __grandmother__. My father's mother is my

   _____, too.

2. My mother's father is my _____. My mother's brother is my

   _____. My mother's sister is my _____.

3. My brother's son is my _____. My brother's daughter is my _____.

4. My husband's brother is my _____. My husband's sister is my

   _____.

5. My grandmother's daughter is my _____ or my _____.

6. My grandfather's son is my _____ or my _____.

7. My father's daughter is my _____ or _____.

8. My mother's son is my _____ or _____.

BONUS POINTS: What's a step-sister? a great-grandmother? a cousin?

3 BELONGINGS Grammar Notes 1–5

Change the possessive nouns to possessive adjectives.

Her
1. ~~Carol's~~ school is in Oregon.

2. The cats' food is in a bowl.

3. Pete's mother is in Florida.

4. Yoko's teacher is Al Brown.

5. The dog's fur is brown.

6. Elenore and Pete's apartment is in New York City.

7. My mother-in-law's home is in London.

8. The girls' bicycles are in the garage.

4 QUESTIONS Grammar Note 6

Complete the questions. Use **where's**, **who's**, **whose**, *and* **what's**.

1. _____ his last name? It's Winston.

2. _____ in the kitchen? Mom is.

3. _____ books are on the floor? Carol's.

4. _____ your homework? It's at home.

5 BERTHA BEAN'S FAMILY Grammar Note 3

Complete the sentences. Use subject pronouns and possessive adjectives.

_____My_____ name is Bertha Bean. _____I_____ live in Florida.
1. 2.

_____ am a widow. I have two children, a son and a
3.

daughter. _____ son is a police
4.
officer. _____ is forty years
5.
old. _____ name is Jack.
6.
_____ wife is a nurse. They
7.

live in Connecticut. They have three

children. _____ children are seven, six, and three years old.
8.

My daughter is a teacher. _____ is thirty-three years old.
9.

_____ is single. _____ home is in Boston. _____ lives near
10. 11. 12.

Lulu Winston's granddaughter Norma. _____ daughter and Lulu's
13.

granddaughter are neighbors. Lulu and I are neighbors and friends.

COMMUNICATION PRACTICE

6 FAMILY TREES

Draw your family tree. Then work in small groups. Tell your group about different people in your family.

EXAMPLE:

Woo Hyun Lee is my mother's brother. He's my favorite uncle. He's a businessman. He's in the United States now. He's a strong and intelligent man.

7 GAME: WHOSE BROTHER IS THIS?

Bring in photos of family members. Write how the person is related to you on the back of the photo (my sister, my mother, my aunt, etc.). The teacher collects the photos and gives each student a photo. Students ask questions about the photos.

EXAMPLE:

STUDENT 1: Whose _____sister_____ is this?

STUDENT 2: I think it's Juan's.

JUAN: You're right. She's my sister. *(Now Juan asks a question.)*

8 FIND SOMEONE WHOSE __ / FIND SOMEONE WHO'S __

*Complete the questions. Use **whose** or **who's**. Then ask your classmates these questions. Write their answers.*

1. ___Whose___ birthday is in February? _____Juan's is._____

2. _____ good in art? _____

3. _____ handwriting is beautiful? _____

4. _____ a good athlete? _____

5. _____ eyes are green? _____

6. _____ a good cook? _____

7. _____ first name is long? (eight or more letters) _____

8. _____ book bag is heavy? _____

9. _____ birthday is in the summer? _____

10. _____ a good dancer? _____

QUESTIONS WITH *WHEN* AND *WHAT* + NOUN; PREPOSITIONS; ORDINAL NUMBERS

GRAMMAR **IN CONTEXT**

WARM UP   What is your favorite holiday? When is it?

Listen and read the conversation between Doug and his friends Noah and Dino.

NOAH: Hey Doug.

DOUG: Hey Noah, Dino. How're you doing?

NOAH: Okay. And you?

DOUG: Good. By the way, what's the next school holiday?

NOAH: Election Day.

DOUG: **When** is it?

NOAH: It's **on** the **first** Tuesday in November.

DINO: Not always.

NOAH: Yes it is.

DINO: No it's not.

DOUG: Then **what day** is Election Day?

DINO: Election Day is **on** the **first** Tuesday after the **first** Monday **in** November. This year it's *not* **on** the **first** Tuesday **in** November.

NOAH: Okay, okay. You're such a genius.

GRAMMAR **PRESENTATION**

WHEN

WHEN	VERB	
When	is	Independence Day?

ANSWERS

It's on July 4th.
On July 4th.
July 4th.

WHAT + NOUN

WHAT	NOUN	VERB	OBJECT
What	day	is	the party?
What	time	is	the party?

ANSWERS

It's on Monday.
On Monday.
Monday.

It's at 8:00.
At 8:00.
8:00.

PREPOSITIONS OF TIME

Her graduation is	**in** December. **in** (the) winter. **in** 1999. **in** the morning. **in** the afternoon. **in** the evening.
Is your birthday	**on** Wednesday? **on** December 25th?
The party is	**at** 7:30. **at** night.

ORDINAL NUMBERS

1st = first	12th = twelfth	32nd = thirty-second
2nd = second	13th = thirteenth	40th = fortieth
3rd = third	14th = fourteenth	43rd = forty-third
4th = fourth	15th = fifteenth	50th = fiftieth
5th = fifth	16th = sixteenth	60th = sixtieth
6th = sixth	17th = seventeenth	70th = seventieth
7th = seventh	18th = eighteenth	80th = eightieth
8th = eighth	19th = nineteenth	90th = ninetieth
9th = ninth	20th = twentieth	100th = hundredth
10th = tenth	21st = twenty-first	101st = one hundred first
11th = eleventh	30th = thirtieth	

NOTES	**EXAMPLES**
1. Use *when* or *what* **+ noun** for questions about time.	• **When** is your party? It's on Tuesday. • **What day** is your party? It's on Tuesday.

2. We usually use **prepositions** when we answer questions about time. *in* + months, seasons, years *in* + *the morning, the afternoon, the evening* *on* + days of the week *on* + the date *at* + the exact time *at* + *night*	• It's **in** January. • Her graduation was **in** 1999. • My son is at camp **in the afternoon**. • It's **on** Monday and Wednesday. • It's **on** January 4. • It's **at** ten o' clock **in the morning** and **at** eight o' clock **at night**.

3. There are two kinds of numbers: **cardinal**—*one, two three*. **ordinal**—*first, second, third*. Use **ordinal numbers** for dates, streets, and floors of a building.	• She has **three** classes on Thursday. • Her **first** class is at 9:00. • His birthday is on January **twentieth**. OR • It's on January **20th**. • Her apartment is on **Seventy-seventh** Street. OR • It's on **77th** Street.

4. Use **ordinal numbers** to number things in a sequence. The spelled form is used.	• Her **first** class is English. Her **second** is math. Her **third** class is history. NOT ~~Her 1st class is English.~~

REFERENCE NOTE
See Appendix 3, pages A-3 and A-4, for a list of cardinal and ordinal numbers.
See Appendix 3, pages A-3 and A-4, for a list of the days, months, and seasons.
See Appendix 4, page A-4, for information about telling time.

FOCUSED PRACTICE

1 DISCOVER THE GRAMMAR

MAY

SUNDAY	MONDAY	TUESDAY	WEDNESDAY	THURSDAY	FRIDAY	SATURDAY
	1	2	3	4	5	6
7	8 Meet Denise at New Age Tea	9	10	11 Book group, 7 P.M.	12	13
14	15	16	17	18	19	20 Pick up theater tickets
21	22	23	24 10 A.M. Dr. Koren	25	26	27
28	29	30 Writer's Conference 6 to 8 P.M.	31			

JUNE

SUNDAY	MONDAY	TUESDAY	WEDNESDAY	THURSDAY	FRIDAY	SATURDAY
				1	2	3
4	5 Return library books	6	7	8	9	10 Doug's soccer game 2 P.M.
11	12	13	14 Meet with editor for lunch	15	16	17 Wedding Natalie and Les 9 P.M.
18	19	20	21	22	23	24
25	26	27	28	29	30	

Look at Elenore's calendar. Match the occasion, the date, and the time.

Occasion	Date	Time
1. The Writer's Conference is	on June 10	in the afternoon
2. Elenore's doctor's appointment is	on June 17	at night
3. Doug's soccer game is	on May 30	in the morning
4. Natalie and Les' wedding is	on May 24	in the evening

2 SCHEDULE OF EVENTS

A. *Look at Pete's old planner. Complete the conversations. Use* **When**, **What time**, **on**, **at**, *and* **in the**.

WEEKLY PLANNER

◯ **MONDAY**   **January 1st**
                                      NEW YEAR'S DAY

   TUESDAY   **January 2nd**
      meeting with Doug Nagano–10 A.M.
◯   *meeting with Carol Loomis–12:30 P.M.*
      meeting with Art Kantor, Ray Stone, Marilyn Hooper–4 P.M.

   WEDNESDAY   **January 3rd**
      fly to São Paulo– 7 P.M. flight

◯ **THURSDAY**   **January 4th**
      free day

   FRIDAY   **January 5th**
◯   *talk to marketing directors – 2 P.M.*
      talk to communications directors–3:30 P.M.

---

1. **A:** _____ was Pete's meeting with Doug Nagano?

   B: It was _____ January 2nd _____ _____ morning.

2. **A:** _____ was Pete's flight to São Paulo?

   B: It was _____ night.

   A: _____ _____ was it?

   B: It was _____ 7 P.M.

3. **A:** _____ was Pete's talk?

   B: It was _____ January 5th. It was _____ _____ afternoon.

B. *Complete the sentences with* **first**, **second**, *and* **third**.

1. Pete's ____first____ meeting was on January 2nd at 10 A.M. His _____

   meeting was at 12:30 P.M., and his _____ was at 4 P.M.

2. On January 5th, Pete's _____ talk was at 2 P.M. and his _____ talk

   was at 3:30 P.M.

3 WHERE'S THE PARTY? Grammar Notes 3–4

Pete and Elenore are going to a party. They are confused. Listen to their conversation. Then listen again and complete the sentences.

1. John and Sue live _____ Street between _____ and

   _____ Avenue.

2. Their apartment is _____ floor.

3. John and Alice live _____ Street between _____ and

   _____ Avenue.

4. Their apartment is _____ floor.

4 NATIONAL HOLIDAYS Grammar Notes 1–2, 4

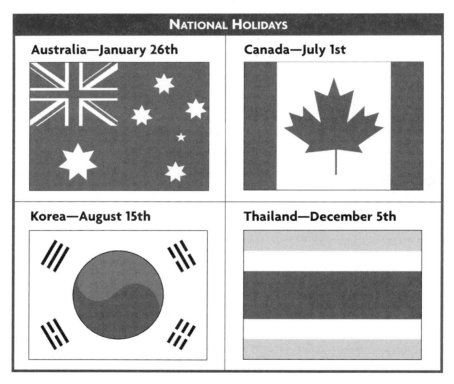

NATIONAL HOLIDAYS	
Australia—January 26th	**Canada—July 1st**
Korea—August 15th	**Thailand—December 5th**

Look at the chart and answer the questions.

1. When is Australia's national holiday? _It's on January 26th._____

2. When is Thailand's national holiday? _____

3. What country's national holiday is on July 1st? _____

4. What country's national holiday is in August? _____

COMMUNICATION PRACTICE

5 INFORMATION GAP: HOLIDAYS AROUND THE WORLD

Work in pairs.

Student A, look at the chart on this page. Ask your partner questions to complete your chart.

Student B, look at the Information Gap on page 105 and follow the instructions there.

EXAMPLES:

What country's national holiday is on _____? (date)

What month is _____'s national holiday?

What's the date of _____'s national holiday?

What country's national holiday is in _____? (month)

When is _____'s national holiday?

NATIONAL HOLIDAYS AROUND THE WORLD					
COUNTRY	**MONTH**	**DAY**	**COUNTRY**	**MONTH**	**DAY**
Argentina		25th	Haiti	January	
Brazil	September		Italy	June	2nd
	April	16th	Japan	December	22nd
Dominican Republic	February	27th	Lebanon	November	22nd
Ecuador	August		Turkey	October	29th
Greece		25th	United States of America	July	4th
Your country's national holiday:					

6 SCHOOL HOLIDAYS

Work in small groups. Look at a school calendar. What are your school's holidays? When are they?

QUESTIONS WITH *WHO, WHOM,* AND *WHY; WH-* QUESTIONS AND THE PRESENT PROGRESSIVE

GRAMMAR IN CONTEXT

WARM UP   Check the kinds of TV shows you like.

comedies	☐	news magazines	☐	movies	☐
medical dramas	☐	news	☐	music videos (MTV)	☐
police dramas	☐	sports	☐		
legal dramas	☐	talk shows	☐	mysteries	☐

What's your favorite TV show? _____

Bertha calls Lulu. Listen and read their conversation.

LULU: Hello.

BERTHA: Hi, Lulu? Bertha. How are you doing?

LULU: So-so. My back is still bothering me.

BERTHA: Gee, I'm sorry to hear that. Is that the TV?

LULU: Yes.

BERTHA: It's very loud. **Where are you watching TV?**

LULU: In my bedroom. The phone is near the TV.

BERTHA: **What are you watching?**

LULU: *Sleepless in Seattle.*

BERTHA: Oh. That was a good movie. I just love romantic comedies. Who's in it again?

LULU: Tom Hanks and Meg Ryan.

BERTHA: Oh yeah. **What's happening?**

LULU: Tom Hanks is asking a woman for a date.

BERTHA: **Who's he asking?** Meg Ryan?

LULU: No. That comes later.

BERTHA: **Why are you watching TV now?** Your photography class is in half an hour.

LULU: Not today. Our teacher is away.

BERTHA: Oh. Well then, enjoy the movie. And feel better.

LULU: Thanks. Bye.

BERTHA: Bye.

GRAMMAR **PRESENTATION**
QUESTIONS WITH *WHO, WHOM,* AND *WHY;*
WH- QUESTIONS AND THE PRESENT PROGRESSIVE

WH- WORD	*BE*	SUBJECT	BASE FORM OF VERB + *-ING*	ANSWERS
Who	is		sleeping?	Lulu is. Lulu is sleeping.
What	is		happening?	I'm cooking for our party.
Who(m)	is	Doug	meeting?	Noah. Doug is meeting Noah.
Why	are	you	hurrying?	I'm late. I'm hurrying because I'm late.
What	are	you	making?	Soup. I'm making soup.
Where	are	they	going?	To the supermarket. They're going to the supermarket.

NOTES

1. Every sentence has a subject and a verb.

Some sentences have a subject, a verb, and an object.

Use *who* to ask questions about the subject.

In informal English, use *who* to ask questions about the object.

In formal English, use *whom* to ask questions about the object.

EXAMPLES

subject verb
• **Lulu is** sleeping.

subject verb   object
• **Lulu is** hugging **Bertha**.

A: **Who** is sleeping?
B: **Lulu** is (sleeping).

A: **Who** is hugging Bertha?
B: **Lulu** is (hugging Bertha).

A: **Who** is Lulu hugging?
B: **Bertha**. (Lulu is hugging **Bertha**.)

A: **Whom** is Professor Walters meeting?
B: **Bekir**. (Professor Walters is meeting **Bekir**.)

2. Use *why* to ask for reasons.

A: Why are they sleeping?

B: They're sleeping because they're tired.

OR

B: Because they're tired. (spoken English)

OR

B: They're tired. (*Because* is understood.)

3. Many *wh-* questions in the **present progressive** use the same word order as *yes / no* questions.

YES / NO QUESTIONS:
- **Are you** cooking?
- Where **are you** cooking?
- Why **are you** cooking?

▶ **BE CAREFUL!** *Who* and *what* questions about the object use *yes / no* question word order.

Who and *what* questions about the subject do not use the same word order as *yes / no* questions.

QUESTIONS ABOUT THE OBJECT:
- Who **are you** meeting?
- What **are you** cooking?

QUESTIONS ABOUT THE SUBJECT:
- Who **is cooking**?
- What **is happening**?

REFERENCE NOTE
See Unit 9 for a discussion of questions with *who, what,* and *where.*

FOCUSED PRACTICE

1 DISCOVER THE GRAMMAR

Read this passage about Milt.

> Milt is visiting his family in Brazil. His sister, Alessandra, is meeting him at the airport. Alessandra is kissing Milt on both cheeks. That's the custom in Brazil.

Match the questions and answers.

<u> d </u> **1.** Where is Milt meeting Alessandra?

_____ **2.** What is Milt doing in Brazil?

_____ **3.** Who is kissing Milt?

_____ **4.** Who is Alessandra kissing?

_____ **5.** Why is Alessandra kissing Milt on both cheeks?

a. Alessandra.

b. Because that's the custom in Brazil.

c. He's visiting his family.

d. At the airport in São Paulo.

e. Milt.

2 WHY IS PETE COOKING FOR AN ARMY? Grammar Notes 1–2

Complete the conversation. Use **what**, **who**, *and* **why**. *Then listen and check your work.*

ELENORE: Gee. It's hot here in the kitchen. _____What_____ are you doing?
                                               1.

PETE: _____ am I doing? I'm cooking.
          2.

ELENORE: Yes, I see. But _____ are you cooking?
                            3.

PETE: I'm making two chickens and pasta with tomato sauce.

ELENORE: You're cooking for an army! _____ are you cooking for?
                                        4.

PETE: I'm cooking for Caroline, Ray, Andrea, Billy, and us.

ELENORE: _____ are you cooking for Caroline, Ray, Andrea, and Billy?
             5.

PETE: I'm preparing for our dinner party.

ELENORE: That's next week.

PETE: No, it isn't. Look at the calendar. It's tonight.

ELENORE: Oh, no! You're right. Is everything ready?

PETE: Are you kidding? Roll up your sleeves.

ELENORE: Yes, sir.

③ EDITING

Correct the questions. Then read Exercise 2 and answer them.

_____ **1.** Who cooking?

    a. Elenore   **b.** Pete

_____ **2.** What Pete is doing?

    a. He's making dinner.   **b.** He's making lunch.

_____ **3.** What he cooking?

    a. Two chickens and pasta with   **b.** Two chickens with mushrooms
        tomato sauce   and rice

_____ **4.** Who is cooking for?

    a. An army   **b.** A few friends

_____ **5.** Where Pete and Elenore are having a conversation?

    a. In the living room   **b.** In the kitchen

_____ **6.** Why Pete is cooking now?

    a. The dinner party is tonight.   **b.** The dinner party is tomorrow night.

④ A BALL GAME   **Grammar Notes 1, 3**

Doug is returning home. He meets his friend, Noah. Noah is wearing headphones. Complete their conversation. Then listen and check your work.

DOUG: Hey Noah. What _____?
                                               1. (listen to)

NOAH: The ball game.

DOUG: Who _____?
                                              2. (play)

NOAH: The Mets are playing the Dodgers.

DOUG: Where _____?
                                             3. (play)

NOAH: In New York.

DOUG: Who _____?
                                             4. (win)

NOAH: It's a tie. It's the bottom of the ninth. Wait . . . Something's happening.
        Everyone's shouting.

DOUG: What _____?
                                                5. (happen)

ANNOUNCER: It's a home run.

NOAH: A home run. Yes! The Mets are winners.

5 A FUNNY TV SHOW

Elenore is sick. Pete is calling her. Listen to their conversation. Then listen again and answer the questions.

1. Who is watching TV?

Elenore is.

2. What program is she watching?

_____

3. Where are Lucy and Ethel working?

_____

4. Is Elenore enjoying the show? _____

5. Who's sneezing? _____

6. Why is this person sneezing? _____

6 A GOODNIGHT STORY FOR DAD

Look at the picture. Write questions in the present progressive. Then answer them.

1. Who / sleep

A: Who is sleeping?

B: The father is.

2. Where / the father / sleep

A: _____

B: _____

3. Who / hold / a book

A: _____

B: _____

4. Who / smile

A: _____

B: _____

5. Why / the little girl / smile

A: _____

B: _____ (father / sleep)

COMMUNICATION PRACTICE

7 INFORMATION GAP: SURFING THE CHANNELS

Work in pairs.

Student A, ask your partner questions to complete sentences 1 and 2.

Student B, turn to the Information Gap on page 104 and follow the directions there.

EXAMPLE:
A: Where is a man lying?
B: He's lying on the floor.

1. **CHANNEL 2:** A man is lying on _____. A _____ is sticking out of

   his chest. _____, _____, _____, and a

   maid are sitting in the living room and talking.

2. **CHANNEL 4:** Some young men are wearing _____. They're _____

   on a playing field. One man is carrying a _____.

3. **CHANNEL 5:** A woman is sitting behind a desk. She is talking about the president's trip
   to Asia.

4. **CHANNEL 7:** A woman is laughing. She's throwing a pie in a man's face.

Now, work with your partner and decide together what kind of show is on each channel.

1. Channel 2 is a _____.

2. Channel 4 is a _____.

3. Channel 5 is a _____.

4. Channel 7 is a _____.

8 WHAT ARE YOU WATCHING?

Prepare a conversation with a partner.

Student A is watching TV when Student B calls. Student B, ask Student A questions about his or her show. Ask questions in the present progressive.

A: Hello.

B: Hi, _____. This is _____.

   Are you busy?

A: Oh hi, _____. I'm _____.
   _(watch)

B: Oh, what's happening?

A: . . .

PART III

REVIEW OR SELFTEST

I. *Read each conversation. Circle the letter of the underlined word or group of words that is not correct.*

1. A: <u>Who's</u> her mother?
          A

    B: Elenore <u>is</u> <u>Carol</u> <u>mother</u>.
              B   C   D

                                                   A B C D

2. A: <u>What</u> <u>day's</u> is your party?
          A   B

    B: <u>It's</u> <u>on</u> Saturday.
           C   D

                                                   A B C D

3. A: <u>When</u> <u>is your class</u>?
          A   B

    B: <u>It's</u> <u>on the afternoon</u>.
           C   D

                                                   A B C D

4. A: <u>Where's</u> the library?
          A

    B: It's <u>near</u> the elevator <u>in the</u> <u>third</u> floor.
             B   C   D

                                                       A B C D

5. A: <u>What</u> <u>you're</u> <u>doing</u>?
          A   B   C

    B: <u>We're</u> watching the news on TV.
         D

                                                   A B C D

II. *Complete the sentences. Choose the correct word.*

1. My classroom is on the _____ floor.
                                    (two, second)

2. My _____ class is at nine-thirty.
          (one, first)

3. Lulu is _____ years old.
        (seventy-three, seventy-third)

4. Her home is on _____ Street.
           (Twenty-nine, Twenty-ninth)

5. November is the _____ month of the year.
               (eleven, eleventh)

III. *Read the invitation. Complete the questions. Use*
who, **what**, **where**, **when**, **whose**.

> ┌─────────────────────────────────────┐
> **BIRTHDAY PARTY**
> **FOR:** Jeff
> **AT:** 350 East 77 Street, Apt. 2A
> **ON:** November 2   **AT:** 9 P.M.
> **RSVP:** Noah at 980-2240
>   or Doug 876-9898
> └─────────────────────────────────────┘

1. _____ is on November 2nd? Jeff's party.

2. _____ birthday party is on November 2nd? Jeff's party.

3. _____ is the party? It's at 350 East 77 Street, Apt. 2A.

4. _____ is the party? It's on November 2nd.

5. _____ time is the party? It's at 9 P.M.

6. _____ is giving the party? Noah and Doug are.

IV. *Write questions about the underlined words.*

1. **A:** _____ ?
   B: Lulu's birthday is <u>on October 15th</u>.

2. **A:** _____ ?
   B: Doug is <u>at home</u>.

3. **A:** _____ ?
   B: Lulu's last name is <u>Winston</u>.

4. **A:** _____ ?
   B: <u>Elenore</u> is reading in the living room.

5. **A:** _____ ?
   B: Lulu is meeting <u>Bertha</u>.

6. **A:** _____ ?
   B: <u>Dan's</u> hat is in the closet.

V. *Cross out the underlined words. Use* **His**, **Her**, **Its**, *or* **Their**.

1. <u>Carol's</u> uncle is a plumber.

2. <u>The Winstons'</u> car is old.

3. <u>Doug's</u> sister Norma is a Spanish teacher.

4. This is my turtle. <u>My turtle's</u> name is Mertle.

5. <u>The students'</u> tests are on the teacher's desk.

▶ *To check your answers, go to the Answer Key on page 104.*

PART III

FROM GRAMMAR TO WRITING PUNCTUATION I: THE APOSTROPHE, THE COMMA, THE PERIOD, THE QUESTION MARK

 1 *Read this e-mail letter. Then circle all the punctuation marks.*

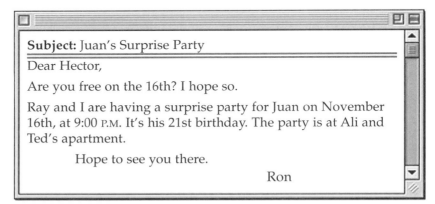

Subject: Juan's Surprise Party

Dear Hector,

Are you free on the 16th? I hope so.

Ray and I are having a surprise party for Juan on November 16th, at 9:00 P.M. It's his 21st birthday. The party is at Ali and Ted's apartment.

Hope to see you there.

Ron

Study these rules of punctuation.

The Apostrophe (')

1. Use an apostrophe to show possession and to write contractions.

- **Carol's** book is here.
- We **aren't** late.

The Comma (,)

2. Rules for commas vary. Here are some places where commas are almost always used:

a. in a list of more than two things

b. after the name of a person you are writing to

c. after *yes* or *no* in a sentence

d. when you use *and* to connect two sentences.

- He is wearing **a shirt, a sweater,** and **a jacket**.

- Dear **John,**

- **Yes,** I am.
  No, I'm not.

- His house is **huge,** and his car is expensive.

The Period (.)

3. a. Use a period at the end of every statement.

b. Use a period after many abbreviations.

- We are English language **students.**

- The party is on **Nov.** 16th.

The Question Mark (?)

4. Use a question mark at the end of a question.

- Are you planning a **party?**
- Where are you **going?**

2 *Add punctuation marks to this note.*

> *Dear Uncle John*
>
> *Bob and I are planning a party for my parents*
> *25th wedding anniversary on Sunday Dec 11th*
> *The party is at our home at 23 Main St Its at*
> *3 o'clock I hope you can make it*
>
> > *Emily*

3 *Write an e-mail to a friend or relative. Invite him or her to a party. Include the following information.*

Who's the party for?
Who's giving the party?
What's the occasion?
When is the party?
Where is the party?

REVIEW OR SELFTEST
ANSWER KEY

PART III

I.
1. C
2. B
3. D
4. C
5. B

II.
1. second
2. first
3. seventy-three
4. Twenty-ninth
5. eleventh

III.
1. What
2. Whose
3. Where
4. When
5. What
6. Who

IV.
1. When is Lulu's birthday (When's Lulu's birthday?)
2. Where is Doug? (Where's Doug?)
3. What is Lulu's last name? (What's Lulu's last name?)
4. Who is reading in the living room? (Who's reading in the living room?)
5. Who is Lulu meeting? (Who's Lulu meeting?)
6. Whose hat is in the closet?

V.
1. ~~Carol's~~ Her
2. ~~The Winstons'~~ Their
3. ~~Doug's~~ His
4. ~~My turtle's~~ Its
5. ~~The students'~~ Their

INFORMATION GAP FOR STUDENT B   Unit 12, Exercise 7

Student B, answer your partner's questions. Then ask your partner questions to complete sentences 3 and 4.

EXAMPLE:
A: Where is a man lying?
B: He's lying on the floor.

1. **CHANNEL 2:** A man is lying on the floor. A knife is sticking out of his chest. The man's wife, a family friend, a detective, and a maid are sitting in the living room and talking.

2. **CHANNEL 4:** Some young men are wearing uniforms. They're running on a playing field. One man is carrying a football.

3. **CHANNEL 5:** A woman is sitting behind _____. She is talking about

   _____ .

4. **CHANNEL 7:** A woman is _____. _____'s throwing a pie in a man's face.

104

Now, work with your partner and decide together what kind of show is on each channel.

1. Channel 2 is a _____ .

2. Channel 4 is a _____ .

3. Channel 5 is a _____ .

4. Channel 7 is a _____ .

INFORMATION GAP FOR STUDENT B   Unit 11, Exercise 5

Student B, answer your partner's questions. Then ask your partner questions to complete your chart.

EXAMPLES:
What country's national holiday is on _____? (date)
What month is _____'s national holiday?
What's the date of _____'s national holiday?
What country's national holiday is in _____? (month)
When is _____'s national holiday?

	NATIONAL HOLIDAYS AROUND THE WORLD						
COUNTRY		**MONTH**	**DAY**	**COUNTRY**		**MONTH**	**DAY**
Argentina		May	25th	Haiti		January	1st
Brazil		September	7th			June	2nd
Denmark		April	16th	Japan		December	
		February	27th	Lebanon			22nd
Ecuador		August	10th			October	29th
Greece		March	25th	United States of America		July	4th
Your country's national holiday:							

THE SIMPLE PRESENT TENSE

PREVIEW

Doug and his mother, Elenore, are shopping for clothes. Listen and read their conversation.

CLOTHES FOR A TEENAGER

DOUG: Mom, look at these jeans.

ELENORE: They're nice, but you have a lot of jeans. You're wearing your favorite ones right now.

DOUG: These? They're way too tight.

ELENORE: But those jeans are very expensive. How about this brand here? These cost half as much.

DOUG: No way. Look at the legs. They're not baggy.

ELENORE: Why do you want baggy jeans?

DOUG: They're cool. All the kids wear them.

ELENORE: Doug, how about one of these nice shirts? You really need a long-sleeved shirt and dress shoes.

DOUG: I don't need a long-sleeved shirt. I have one, and I have dress shoes, too. Besides, I hate dress shoes.

ELENORE: But your long-sleeved shirt has a big stain on it, and your dress shoes are tight.

DOUG: My tie covers the stain, and my shoes are okay because I don't wear socks.

ELENORE: No socks?

DOUG: It's the style. The kids at school don't wear socks.

SALESPERSON: Do you need any help?

DOUG: Yes, I'm looking for baggy jeans like these.

SALESPERSON: What size do you want?

DOUG: My waist is 32.

ELENORE: And he needs a shirt and shoes, too.

SALESPERSON: Well, we have the jeans in size 32. These jeans are comfortable and easy to care for, too. And wait, you're in luck. They're on sale today—$20 off.

DOUG: See, Mom?

SALESPERSON: And we have a big sale on long-sleeved shirts and dress shoes.

ELENORE: See, Doug?

COMPREHENSION CHECK

Check (✔) **That's right**, **That's wrong**, *or* **It doesn't say**.

	That's right.	That's wrong.	It doesn't say.
1. Doug's long-sleeved shirt has a stain.	✔	☐	☐
2. Doug wants to be in style.	✔	☐	☐
3. There are no shoes in size 10.	☐	☐	✔
4. Doug and his mother have the same ideas about clothes.	☐	✔	☐

WHAT'S YOUR OPINION?

Do teenagers usually like to shop with their parents?

WITH PARTNERS

Practice the conversation on pages 106 and 107.

13 SIMPLE PRESENT TENSE: AFFIRMATIVE AND NEGATIVE STATEMENTS

GRAMMAR **IN CONTEXT**

WARM UP   Read the cartoon.

Many people think that clothes are important. What do you think?

 Dr. Kramer is a psychologist. Listen and read a letter to Dr. Kramer.

Dear Dr. Kramer,

My son **is** fourteen years old. He **is** a good student and he **has** many friends. But we **have** one problem with him. He **loves** clothes. He **wants** all the latest styles. We **are** not poor, but I **think** it **is** wrong to spend a lot of money on clothes, especially for a growing boy. We **give** my son money each week, but he **doesn't have** enough to buy all the clothes he **wants**. Now he **wants** to get a part-time job. I **don't want** him to work, but my husband **thinks** it's okay. What **do** you **think**?

Worried Mom

GRAMMAR **PRESENTATION**
SIMPLE PRESENT TENSE: AFFIRMATIVE AND NEGATIVE STATEMENTS

AFFIRMATIVE STATEMENTS		NEGATIVE STATEMENTS		
SUBJECT	**VERB**	**SUBJECT**	***DO NOT / DOES NOT***	**BASE FORM OF VERB**
I You* We They	**work**.	I You* We They	**do not don't**	**work**.
He She It	**works**.	He She It	**does not doesn't**	**work**.

*You is both singular and plural.

NOTES

EXAMPLES

1. Use the **simple present tense** to tell about things that happen again and again (habits, regular occurrences, customs, and routines).

Now

Past ——X————X——+——X————X—— Future
Doug plays soccer every day.

- Doug **plays** soccer every day.
- Many Americans **eat** turkey on Thanksgiving.
- Pete and Elenore **work.**
- Most teenagers **wear** jeans.

2. Use the **simple present tense** to tell **facts**.

- This sweatshirt **costs** thirty dollars.

3. Use the **simple present tense** with **non-action verbs**.

- Doug and his mother **are** in the store.
- Doug **likes** bright colors.

(continued on next page)

4. Use the contractions *doesn't* and *don't* for negative statements in speaking or in informal writing.

- Doug **doesn't** wear ties often. He wears T-shirts.
- We **don't** live in Oregon. We live in New York.

▶ **BE CAREFUL!** When *or* connects two verbs in a negative statement, we do not repeat *don't* or *doesn't* before the second verb.

- He **doesn't work** or **study** in the summer.
- We **don't eat** or **drink** at work. NOT ~~He doesn't work or doesn't study in the summer.~~

5. In affirmative statements, use the **base form** (dictionary form) of the verb for all persons except the third person singular. Put an **-s** (or **-es)** ending on the third person singular (*he / she / it*).

- He need**s** a dress shirt. I need a belt.
- She want**s** an apple. I want bananas.
- He miss**es** me. I miss him.

6. PRONUNCIATION NOTE: Pronounce the third person singular ending /s/, /z/, or /ɪz/.

- /s/ He eat**s** cereal for breakfast.
- /z/ She play**s** basketball.
- /ɪz/ He watch**es** TV every day.

7. The third person singular affirmative forms of *have, do,* and *go* are not regular.

- He **has** a new sweatshirt.
- She **does** the taxes.
- It **goes** in the kitchen.

8. The verb *be* has different forms from all other verbs.

- I **am** tired.
- You **are** tall.
- He **is** bored.
- I **look** tired.
- You **look** tall.
- He **looks** bored.

REFERENCE NOTE
See Unit 26 for a fuller discussion of non-action verbs.
See Appendix 14, page A-14, for spelling and pronunciation rules for the third person singular in the simple present tense.
See Unit 1 for a complete presentation of the verb *be*.

FOCUSED PRACTICE

1 DISCOVER THE GRAMMAR

This is Dr. Kramer's answer to the letter from a worried mom (see page 108). Read the letter and circle the verbs in the simple present tense.

> Dear Worried Mom,
>
> Your son's interest in clothes is not unusual. Most teens want to dress the way their friends dress. As for work, a part-time job is good for a teen as long as his or her schoolwork doesn't suffer. It's good that your son likes to wear nice clothes and wants to work. I agree with your husband. When people work, they usually think carefully about the cost of things. There is no reason to worry. Your son sounds fine to me.
>
> Dr. Kramer

2 LISTENING: VERB ENDINGS   Grammar Note 6

Underline the verb in each sentence. Then listen to the sentences and check the sound of the verb endings. (See Appendix 14, page A-14, for an explanation of these pronunciation rules.)

	/s/	/z/	/ɪz/
1. He <u>wears</u> T-shirts.		✔	
2. He misses his girlfriend.			
3. She plays tennis every week.			
4. She drinks coffee in the morning.			
5. It takes an hour to get to school.			
6. He washes his clothes on Sunday.			
7. She lives in Boston.			
8. He worries about his family.			

3 AL BROWN, AN ENGLISH TEACHER Grammar Notes 1–7

Complete the sentences. Use the correct form of the verb in parentheses.

Al Brown _____teaches_____ English as a
1. (teach)
Second Language. He is unlike the other

teachers in his department. He is only

twenty-seven years old. The other teachers

are over thirty. The other teachers

_____ button-down shirts.
2. (wear)
Al _____ T-shirts or
3. (wear)
sweatshirts. After class the other teachers

_____ home. Every afternoon
4. (go)
Al _____ to the park. Many
5. (go)
students _____ soccer in the
6. (play)
park. Sometimes Al _____ his
7. (watch)
students, and sometimes he

_____ soccer with them.
8. (play)
Three evenings a week Al _____ Japanese lessons with a private tutor. His
9. (have)
tutor is one of his students. Every evening Al _____ Japanese at the library
10. (study)
and _____ Japanese homework.
11. (do)
Al's girlfriend is in Japan. Al _____ her a lot. He _____
12. (miss) 13. (worry)
about her, too. He _____ to see her in the summer.
14. (hope)

*Now circle all the verbs in the third person singular. What three verbs are
pronounced with the extra syllable /ɪz/ in the third person singular?*

_____, _____, and _____

🔊 *Listen and check your work.*

4 WHAT'S THE STORY?   Grammar Notes 3–8

 Listen to the conversation between Doug and his mother. Check (✔) what their conversation is about.

_____ **1.** Elenore is worried about Doug. He is sick. He has a lot of health problems. It's a holiday, and it's hard to find a doctor.

_____ **2.** Doug says he's sick because he doesn't want to go to school. He doesn't remember that it's a holiday and school is closed.

_____ **3.** Doug is sick. He has a headache, a stomachache, and an earache. He wants to go to school because it's a holiday and school is fun on holidays.

5 EDITING

Find and correct the mistakes in this story about Doug.

My name is Doug Winston. I'm in my second year of high school. I'm captain of my
school's soccer team. I ~~lives~~ ^{live} in New York City with my parents. We ~~lives~~ ^{live} in a large
apartment in an old building. Both my mother and father works. My mother is a writer.
She writes stories for magazines. My father is a businessman. His work take him all over
the world. I has two older sisters, Carol and Norma. Carol lives in Oregon and Norma live
in Massachusetts. I no have any brothers. Carol's a student at Oregon State University and
Norma's a Spanish teacher in a high school in Boston. Norma's a good Spanish teacher,
but I'm glad she no is my teacher. She gives her students a lot of homework.

COMMUNICATION PRACTICE

6 MY PARTNER AND I

Check (✔) the sentences that are true for you.

1. _____ I eat breakfast every day.   _____ I don't eat breakfast every day.

2. _____ I speak English after class.   _____ I don't speak English after class.

3. _____ I read in bed.   _____ I don't read in bed.

4. _____ I eat in bed.   _____ I don't eat in bed.

5. _____ I sing in the shower.   _____ I don't sing in the shower.

6. _____ I like big cities.   _____ I don't like big cities.

7. _____ I like leather jackets.   _____ I don't like leather jackets.

8. _____ I like modern art.   _____ I don't like modern art.

9. _____ I like computers.   _____ I don't like computers.

Work with a partner. In what ways are you and your partner alike? In what ways are you different? Write five sentences about you and your partner.

EXAMPLES:

We both eat breakfast every day.

He speaks English after class, but I don't.

7 WEEKEND ACTIVITIES

Listen as each student tells about his or her weekend activities. Take notes. Tell about each student's activities before you tell about your own.

EXAMPLE:

MARIA: On the weekends, I sleep late. I don't go to school.

BEKIR: On the weekends, Maria sleeps late. She doesn't go to school. I work. I don't eat breakfast at home.

CARLOS: Maria sleeps late and she doesn't go to school. Bekir works. He doesn't eat breakfast at home. I play tennis. I don't study.

⑧ INFORMATION GAP: CUSTOMS AROUND THE WORLD

Work in pairs.

Student A, complete sentences 1–4.

Then read sentences 1–4 to your partner. Your partner says "That's right" or corrects your sentence. Your partner reads sentences 5–8 to you. Listen and say "That's right" or correct your partner's sentence.

Student B, look at the Information Gap on page 147 and follow the instructions there.

1. People in Japan _____ shoes in their home. When they enter a home,
   a. (wear / don't wear)

   they _____ their shoes and _____ slippers.
   b. (remove / don't remove)   c. (put on / don't put on)

2. People in Korea _____ rice cake soup on New Year's Day. Children
   a. (eat / don't eat)

   often _____ red jackets with sleeves of many colors.
   b. (wear / don't wear)

3. People in Thailand bow to show respect. Younger people usually

   _____ first.
   a. (bow / don't bow)

4. In Brazil during Carnival people wear strange and beautiful costumes. Brazilians

   _____ during Carnival. They _____ in the street.
   a. (work / don't work)   b. (dance / don't dance)

5. In Saudi Arabia at the time of Ramadan, Moslems don't eat or drink during daylight.

   Ramadan lasts for thirty days. At the end of Ramadan there is a three-day celebration.

6. On New Year's Day, Chinese children receive money in red envelopes from their

   parents and grandparents.

7. In the United States, people usually don't work on July 4th. They watch fireworks

   and have barbecues.

8. In Denmark, people bang on their friends' doors and set off fireworks on New Year's Eve.

Now work with your partner. Write about customs you know well. Read your sentences to the class.

_____

_____

_____

_____

14 SIMPLE PRESENT TENSE: YES / NO QUESTIONS AND SHORT ANSWERS

GRAMMAR IN CONTEXT

WARM UP Look at these ads for roommates. What information is important in a roommate ad?

> **ROOMMATE WANTED**
> Female artist and non-smoker is looking to share large one-bedroom apartment. Inexpensive.
> **Call 689-9069**

> **ROOMMATE NEEDED**
> Male law student looking for roommate to share a small two-bedroom apartment. Quiet location.
> **Call 249-0087**

 Listen and read this roommate questionnaire and Dan and Jon's answers.

ROOMMATE QUESTIONNAIRE

Names:	Dan YES	Dan NO	Jon YES	Jon NO
1. **Do** you **smoke**?		✓		✓
2. **Does** the smell of smoke bother you?	✓			✓
3. **Do** you **wake up** early?		✓		✓
4. **Do** you **like** to go to bed after midnight?	✓		✓	
5. Are you neat?	✓		✓	
6. **Does** a messy room bother you?	✓		✓	
7. Are you quiet?		✓	✓	
8. Are you talkative?	✓			✓
9. **Do** you **listen** to loud music?	✓		✓	
10. **Do** you **watch** a lot of TV?	✓		✓	
11. **Do** you **study** and **listen** to music at the same time?	✓		✓	
12. **Do** you **study** with the TV on?	✓		✓	

WHAT'S YOUR OPINION?

Are Dan and Jon a good match?

Yes ☐ No ☐

GRAMMAR **PRESENTATION**
SIMPLE PRESENT TENSE: *YES / NO* QUESTIONS AND SHORT ANSWERS

YES / NO QUESTIONS		
DO / DOES	**SUBJECT**	**BASE FORM OF VERB**
Do	I you* we they	**work**?
Does	he she it	

SHORT ANSWERS			
	AFFIRMATIVE		
Yes,	I you* we they	**do**.	
	he she it	**does**.	

SHORT ANSWERS			
	NEGATIVE		
No,	I you* we they	**don't**.	
	he she it	**doesn't**.	

*You is both singular and plural.

NOTES

EXAMPLES

1. For *yes / no* questions in the simple present tense, use *do* or *does* before the subject. Use the base form of the verb after the subject.

-        subject
  Do you **work**?
- **Does** he **speak** Italian?

2. Do not use *do* or *does* for *yes / no* questions with *be*.

- Do you speak French? **Are** you from France?
- Does he speak French? **Is** he from France?
- Do I know you? **Am** I in the right room?

> **REFERENCE NOTE**
> See Unit 2 for a discussion of *yes / no* questions with *be*.

FOCUSED PRACTICE

1 DISCOVER THE GRAMMAR

Read about Dan and Jon. They're college roommates.

In many ways Dan and Jon are alike. Both Dan and Jon like music and sports, but Dan likes popular music and Jon likes jazz. Both Dan and Jon like basketball, but Jon likes football and Dan doesn't. Dan and Jon are neat. They don't like a messy room. They both like to go to bed late—well after midnight. They watch about two hours of TV at night and they study with the TV on. But in one way Dan and Jon are completely different. Dan is very talkative, but Jon is very quiet. Dan says, "We're lucky about that. It works out very nicely. I talk, he listens." Jon says, "Uh-huh."

Match the questions and answers.

_____ **1.** Do they both like music and sports?

_____ **2.** Do they like to go to bed early?

_____ **3.** Does Dan like popular music?

_____ **4.** Dan is talkative and Jon is quiet. Does it matter?

_____ **5.** Do Dan and Jon like classical music?

a. It doesn't say.

b. Yes, they do.

c. Yes, he does.

d. No, they don't.

e. No, it doesn't.

2 AT A DEPARTMENT STORE Grammar Notes 1–2

Doug is buying a jacket at a department store. Write the correct questions to complete the conversation.

> **a. Do you want to see anything else?**
> **b. Do you have any winter jackets?**
> **c. Do you need any help?**
> **d. Does this jacket come in brown?**

SALESPERSON: ___Do you need any help___?
1.

DOUG: Yes, please. _____?
2.

SALESPERSON: Yes, we do. All our jackets are over there.

DOUG: _____?
3.

SALESPERSON: Let me check. . . . Uh . . . yes. What size are you?

DOUG: Large.

SALESPERSON: Here you go. _____?
4.

DOUG: No thanks.

❸ HOW MUCH IS IT?

Complete the **yes / no** *questions. Then look at the picture and answer the questions.*

1. ___Do___ the pants cost

   thirty dollars?

   ___Yes, they do_____.

2. _____ the pants expensive?

   _____.

3. _____ the jacket cost three

   hundred and fifty dollars?

   _____.

4. _____ the jacket expensive?

   _____.

❹ LEAVING FOR SCHOOL

Doug is leaving for school. Listen to the conversation between Doug and his mother. Then answer the questions with **Yes, he does**, **No, he doesn't**, *or* **I don't know.**

1. Does Doug have his keys?

   ___Yes, he does_____.

2. Does Doug have his book bag?

   _____.

3. Does Doug have his lunch?

   _____.

4. Does Doug have his wallet?

   _____.

5. Does Doug have his soccer shoes? _____.

6. Does Doug have a good day at school? _____.

COMMUNICATION PRACTICE

5 FIND SOMEONE WHO . . .

Find out about your classmates. Ask these questions or add your own. Take notes.
Tell the class something new about a classmate.

Do you _____?

> speak more than two languages
> watch more than three hours of TV every day
> cook well
> know tai chi
> know sign language
> play a musical instrument
> have more than four sisters or brothers
> ski
> fly a plane

Your questions:

_____

_____

Are you _____?

> an only child
> a good dancer
> good at computers
> good at art
> good at sports

Your questions:

_____

_____

Tell the class some things about a classmate.

EXAMPLE:
Claudia speaks three languages. She speaks Spanish, French, and
English. She knows tai chi, but she doesn't know tae kwon do.
She's good at computers, but she's not a good dancer.

6 A TREASURE HUNT

Work in small groups. Ask each other questions. Check (✔) the items you have that are listed in the box. The first group to check ten items wins.

EXAMPLE:
Do you have a mirror?
> OR

Does anyone have a mirror?

a metal watchband	keys	large earrings
a silver ring	a photo of a man with a mustache	tissues
a comb		leather boots
a library card	sunglasses	a red dictionary
a driver's license	a stamp	black shoelaces
a mirror	a leather belt	

7 FACTS ABOUT THE WORLD

*Complete the questions with **Do, Does, Is,** or **Are**. Then work with a partner and answer the questions. Check your answers on page 146.*

1. _____ Canada north of the United States? _____

2. _____ Canada have a king? _____

3. _____ Canada have ten provinces? _____

4. _____ Thailand have a king? _____

5. _____ Thailand famous for its silk? _____

6. _____ Brazilians speak Portuguese? _____

7. _____ Brasília the capital of Brazil? _____

8. _____ Switzerland have two official languages? _____

9. _____ many people in Korea eat kimche? _____

10. _____ kimche spicy? _____

11. _____ Mexico north of Texas? _____

12. _____ tacos popular in Mexico? _____

SIMPLE PRESENT TENSE: *WH*- QUESTIONS

GRAMMAR **IN CONTEXT**

WARM UP The owl is a bird that hunts at night. We call people who like to stay up late at night "night owls." Night owls feel awake at night. Other people are "early birds." They like the early morning hours. They feel awake and eager to work in the morning. Are you a night owl or an early bird?

Look at the picture of Doug and Elenore. Listen and read the questions and guess the answers.

_____ 1. **Who likes** to get up early?

_____ 2. **Who does** Elenore **wake up**?

_____ 3. **What time does** Doug first **wake up**?

_____ 4. **When does** Doug **get up**?

_____ 5. **Why does** Doug **run** to the bus stop?

_____ 6. **What does** Elenore **say** to Doug?

Now listen and read about Doug and his mother.

A NIGHT OWL AND AN EARLY BIRD

Doug Winston, a night owl, hates to get up in the morning. On weekends and vacations, Doug goes to bed after 1:00 A.M. and gets up at noon. Unfortunately for Doug, school starts at 8:15, and Doug needs to get up early.

At 7:00 A.M. Doug's alarm rings. He wakes up, but he doesn't get up. He stays in bed and daydreams. He thinks about his friends, his schoolwork, and his soccer games. At 7:20 his mother comes in. She has a big smile on her face. She's cheerful and full of energy. She says, "Dougie, it's time to get up."

Elenore, Doug's mom, is an early bird. Even on vacations, Elenore is up at 6:00 A.M. When Elenore wakes Doug in the morning, he moans and groans. He's a grouch in the morning. He says, "Go away. Leave me alone. I'm tired. I need more sleep."

Finally, at about 7:30 Doug gets up. He jumps out of bed, showers, and gets dressed. At 7:50 he drinks a big glass of orange juice, takes a donut, and runs to the bus stop.

Now match the questions on page 122 with the answers.

a. He doesn't want to be late.

b. Doug.

c. At 7:30.

d. "Dougie, it's time to get up."

e. Elenore.

f. At 7:00.

GRAMMAR **PRESENTATION**

SIMPLE PRESENT TENSE: *WH-* QUESTIONS

WH- QUESTIONS				
WH- WORD	*DO / DOES*	SUBJECT	BASE FORM OF VERB	
1. **What**		I	**do**	after breakfast?
2. **Where**	**do**	you	**eat**	lunch?
3. **When**		we	**leave**	work?
4. **What time**		they	**come**	home?
5. **Why**	**does**	he	**live**	in New York?
6. **Who(m)**		she	**call**	on Sunday?

ANSWERS
1. You get dressed after breakfast.
2. I eat lunch in the school cafeteria.
3. We leave work at 5:00.
4. They come home at 6:00.
5. He lives in New York because he works there.
6. She calls her mother on Sunday.

SHORT ANSWERS
1. You get dressed.
2. In the school cafeteria.
3. At 5:00.
4. At 6:00.
5. He works there.
6. Her mother.

WH- QUESTIONS ABOUT THE SUBJECT		
WH- WORD	VERB	
Who	**wears**	sweatshirts?
What	**costs**	a lot?

ANSWERS
Doug's friends (do).
Doug's sweatshirt (does).

NOTES

1. *Wh-* **questions** give information and cannot be answered with a *yes* or *no*.

EXAMPLES

A: **What** does he need?
B: He needs some milk.

2. Most *wh-* questions in the simple present begin with a question word followed by *do* or *does* followed by the subject and the base form of the verb.

- **When do you eat** breakfast?
- **Where does she live?**
- **What does it mean?**
- **Why do we dream?**
- **How do I get** there?
- **Who does he love?**

3. Do not use *do* or *does* when *who* or *what* begins a question about the subject.

subject
- Noah speaks Spanish.
  Who speaks Spanish?
  NOT ~~Who does speak Spanish?~~
- Twenty comes after nineteen.
  What comes after nineteen?
  NOT ~~What does come after nineteen?~~

4. Always use the third person singular form of the verb when *who* or *what* begins a question about the subject.

- Who **speaks** Spanish?
  Pedro does.
- Who **speaks** Korean?
  Eun Joo and Sun-Keun do.
- What **comes** before *d*?
  A, b, and *c* do.

5. *Who* asks questions about a subject.

Who asks questions about an object in informal English.

Whom asks questions about the object in formal English.

subject
- **Doug** plays soccer.
  Who plays soccer? **Doug** does.

object
- Doug meets **Noah** at the park.
  Who does Doug meet? **Noah.**

object
- The king greets **his guests**.
  Whom does the King greet?

PRONUNCIATION NOTE
In pronunciation we use falling intonation for *wh-* questions: Where do you live?

FOCUSED PRACTICE

① DISCOVER THE GRAMMAR

It's eight o'clock on a Monday morning. Dan and Carol are in a math class. Read their conversation. Then match the questions with the answers.

DAN: Am I tired! (yawning)

CAROL: I can see that.

DAN: I always have trouble getting to an eight o'clock class, especially on Monday.

CAROL: That's because you sleep until noon on Sunday and stay up late on Sunday night. Do you ever have trouble falling asleep?

DAN: Yes. But then I read our math book. That puts me to sleep.

_____ **1.** Who sleeps until noon on Sunday?

_____ **2.** What day is it especially hard to get to an eight o'clock class?

_____ **3.** Why does Dan have trouble waking up early on Monday?

_____ **4.** When does Dan sleep until noon?

_____ **5.** What does Dan do when he wants to fall asleep?

a. Monday.

b. Sunday.

c. He reads his math book.

d. Because he stays up late on Sunday.

e. Dan.

What do you do when you have trouble falling asleep?

② DOUG'S DAY   Grammar Notes 1–5

Read each sentence. Write a question that the underlined words answer.

1. Doug wakes up <u>at 7:00</u>.

    When does Doug wake up?

2. Doug's school begins <u>at 8:15</u>.

3. Doug eats lunch <u>in the school cafeteria</u>.

4. Doug eats <u>a hamburger and french fries</u> for lunch on Mondays.

5. Doug and Noah go <u>to the park</u> after school.

_____

6. Doug and Noah meet <u>Dino and Jeff</u> at the park.

_____

7. <u>Doug</u> plays soccer in the park.

_____

8. Doug practices soccer every day <u>because he is the captain of his team and soccer is important to him</u>.

_____

3 **LULU**

Label the **subject (S)** *and the* **object (O)** *in each sentence. Write one question about the subject and one question about the object. Then answer the questions. Use short answers.*

                                  S   O

1. On Sunday afternoon, Pete calls Lulu in Florida.

    Who calls Lulu in Florida on Sunday afternoon? Pete does.

    Who does Pete call on Sunday afternoon? Lulu.

2. Lulu visits Bertha almost every afternoon.

_____

_____

3. Lulu meets her neighbor every Tuesday morning.

_____

_____

4. The neighbor helps Lulu with her grocery shopping.

_____

_____

5. Lulu and Bertha meet Adele and Edith at a restaurant every Monday evening.

_____

_____

4 **DREAMS**

Use these words to write questions. Then read this magazine article about dreams and answer the questions.

1. Who / dream   Who dreams _____?

_____ Everyone dreams. _____

2. Why / people / dream _____?

_____

3. When / people / dream _____?

_____

4. What / psychologists / believe about dreams _____?

   a. _____

   b. _____

   c. _____

5. What / dreams / prove _____?

_____

Dreams ☆

Why do we dream? Nobody knows, but everyone dreams. We dream during REM (rapid eye movement) sleep. In eight hours of sleep, people usually have four REM periods. But we remember very little. We usually remember only 20 or 30 seconds of REM sleep.

There are many ideas about dreams. Some psychologists believe we dream because we need a safe way to do things we can't do when we're awake. Some think we dream in order to work out our problems. Others believe dreams don't have any special meaning. They are simply thoughts that come to us when we sleep. Whatever you believe, dreams prove one thing—some people have wonderful imaginations.

COMMUNICATION PRACTICE

5 MORNING AND NIGHT

Work with a partner. Ask questions about your partner's night and weekday mornings. Tell the class two things about your partner.

EXAMPLES:
Do you dream?
If yes, what do you dream about?
When does your alarm clock ring?
Are you a morning person?
What do you usually have for breakfast?

Now write three questions for a class survey. Report the results.

EXAMPLES:
1. What do you drink in the morning?
2. What do you dream about?

Survey Results:
Six students drink coffee. Two students drink tea. One student drinks milk.

6 HOUSEHOLD CHORES

Study the household chores. Then work with a partner. Ask your partner who does what in his or her home.

EXAMPLES:
A: Who does the dishes in your home?
B: My brother does the dishes.

Household Chores

do the dishes

vacuum

take out the garbage

fix things around the house

cook

make the bed

set the table

7 TRIVIA TIME

Work in groups. Decide together on the correct answer. Check your answers on page 146.

1. Where in Canada do most people speak French?

   a. in Toronto

   b. in Quebec

   c. in Vancouver

2. What famous performing arts center lies on a harbor of the South Pacific Ocean? (some say it looks like a folded dinner napkin)

   a. the Vienna Staatsoper

   b. the Kennedy Center for the Performing Arts

   c. the Sydney Opera House

3. What Southeast Asian city has floating markets early every morning?

   a. Bali

   b. Bangkok

   c. Taiwan

4. Where do bonsai trees, kabuki theater, sumo wrestling, and kendo come from?

   a. Korea

   b. Japan

   c. Mongolia

5. When do most Parisians go on vacation?

   a. in August

   b. in April

   c. in December

6. What European city offers romantic boat rides with singing gondoliers?

   a. Vienna

   b. Verona

   c. Venice

*Now work with a partner. Write your own **wh- questions**. Then ask the class your questions.*

1. _____

2. _____

3. _____

SIMPLE PRESENT TENSE AND
THIS / THAT / THESE / THOSE

GRAMMAR **IN CONTEXT**

WARM UP   Discuss this question.

Is it difficult for you to throw away letters? books? clothes? CDs?

Elenore is trying to clean a closet. Listen and read the conversation.

ELENORE: Pete, please look at the clothes in **that** box. I want to throw
away a few things. Our closet is very full.

PETE: Okay. Elenore! **This** is my favorite sweater. I love **this** sweater.

ELENORE: **That** old thing? You never wear it, and it has a big stain.

PETE: I like it a lot.

ELENORE: Okay. Anything else?

PETE: Yes. I want to keep **these** shoes and **these** pants.

ELENORE: Why? **Those** shoes are tight, and **those** pants have holes.

PETE: Doug wants them.

ELENORE: No, he doesn't.

PETE: Well, I want them.

ELENORE: Okay. Anything else?

PETE: Yes—**this** old hat. I know I don't wear it and it has a hole and
some stains, but it has some wonderful memories.

ELENORE: You win. Let's get a new closet.

PETE: That's a great idea. Now please put everything back.

GRAMMAR **PRESENTATION**
SIMPLE PRESENT TENSE AND *THIS / THAT / THESE / THOSE*

SINGULAR		
THIS / THAT	**VERB**	
This	is	my uncle.
That	's	my jacket.

PLURAL		
THESE / THOSE	**VERB**	
These	are	my friends.
Those		my gloves.

SINGULAR			
THIS / THAT	**NOUN**	**VERB**	
This	man	comes	from Rome.
That	book	has	300 pages.

PLURAL			
THESE / THOSE	**NOUN**	**VERB**	
These	women	are	lawyers.
Those	dictionaries		heavy.

NOTES	EXAMPLES
1. Use *this*, *that*, *these*, and *those* to identify persons or things.	• **Soup** is delicious. *(all soup)* • **This** soup is delicious. *(the soup I'm eating)*
2. *This* refers to a person or thing near you. *That* refers to a person or thing far from you. Use *this* and *that* to talk about a singular noun.	**A:** **This** is my umbrella. **That's** your umbrella by the door. **B:** Oh, sorry. They're both green.
3. *These* refers to people or things near you. *Those* refers to people or things far away. Use *these* and *those* to talk about plural nouns.	**A:** **These** sweaters are not on sale. **B:** **Those** sweaters in the store window are on sale.
4. *This*, *that*, *these*, and *those* can be pronouns or adjectives.	pronoun • **This** is my book. adjective • **This** book is red.

FOCUSED PRACTICE

1 DISCOVER THE GRAMMAR

Lulu is at a new laundromat. She has a problem. Listen and read the conversation between Lulu and the woman who works at the laundromat. Underline **this**, **that**, **these**, *and* **those**. *Circle the nouns they refer to.*

WOMAN: Is something wrong?

LULU: Yes.

WOMAN: What's the problem?

LULU: Well, this isn't my blouse, and these aren't my socks.

WOMAN: Oh, I'm sorry.

LULU: And this isn't my towel. This towel is yellow. My towels are blue. Those towels over there on that shelf look like my towels. And my brown blouse isn't here.

WOMAN: Oh, no. I don't know what happened.

LULU: And look at these pants. They're size 4. Look at me. Am I size 4? I'm not size 4. I'm size 14.

WOMAN: I'm terribly sorry.

LULU: I am, too.

2 A BABYSITTING JOB   Grammar Notes 1–4

Carol's babysitting for Billy, her history professor's son. Carol is taking Billy home from kindergarten. Carol is holding gloves, a jacket, and a scarf. Complete the conversation. Use **this**, **that**, **these**, *or* **those**.

CAROL: Hi, Billy, are you ready to go?

BILLY: Hi, Carol. Look, Carol, ____these____ are my paintings.
                                        1.

CAROL: They're beautiful.

BILLY: Thanks. _____ one is for Mommy, _____ one is for Daddy, and
                        2.   3.
_____ four paintings are for you.
      4.

CAROL: Well, thank you. You're very generous. Billy, are _____ your gloves?
                                                                5.

BILLY: No, they're not. _____ are my gloves under the table.
                              6.

(continued on next page)

CAROL: Okay, Billy, get your gloves. Billy, is

_____ your jacket?

7.

BILLY: Yes, it has my name in it.

CAROL: Is _____ your scarf?

8.

BILLY: No, _____'s my scarf over there.

9.

CAROL: Okay. Now let's hurry home.

BILLY: Okay.

---

3 EDITING

There are five mistakes in these conversations. The first one is corrected. Find and correct the other four.

1. **CAROL:** Helen, ~~this~~ these are my friends Dan and Bob, and this is my roommate Yoko.

   HELEN: Nice to meet you.

2. **ELENORE:** Look at ~~these~~ those men across the street. I think they're famous.

   VALERIE: I think you're right. Those man looks like Tom Cruise. And that one looks

   like Steven Spielberg.

3. **NOAH:** Who are ~~that boys~~ those near the pizza place? Are they from our school?

   DOUG: I can't tell. They're too far away.

4. **ELENORE:** Is ~~these~~ those your earring?

   VALERIE: Yes, it is. Thanks.

COMMUNICATION PRACTICE

4 A NEW LANGUAGE

Are you tired of English? Learn a few words in a new language. Work in small groups. One person in your group probably knows a language that the others don't. Your new language "teacher" points to objects in the room. He or she teaches you vocabulary in the new language. Use **this**, **that**, **these**, *or* **those**.

EXAMPLES:

This is *a door* in English. In French, it's *une porte*.

These are *keys* in English. In Spanish, they're *llaves*.

That's *a window* in English. In Japanese, it's a 家 or まど (pronounced "mado").

Those are *chairs* in English. In Russian, they're стул∧ (pronounced "stool ya").

5 INFORMAL AND FORMAL INTRODUCTIONS

Read the two conversations. Which conversation is more formal—A or B?

Conversation A

CAROL: These are my friends Bill and Steve.

AMY: Hi. I'm Amy.

BILL: Hi, Amy. Nice to meet you.

STEVE: Hi.

AMY: Nice to meet you, too.

Conversation B

PETE: Bill, this is Sam Jones. He's the new director of finance. Mr. Jones, this is Bill Smith. He's our marketing director.

SAM JONES: It's a pleasure to meet you.

BILL SMITH: Nice to meet you, too.

Now, with a partner, practice making informal and formal introductions. Use your own names.

UNIT

17

SIMPLE PRESENT TENSE AND
ONE / ONES AND IT

GRAMMAR **IN CONTEXT**

WARM UP   Read this story. What do you think of it?

A man gets a new umbrella and decides to throw away his old **one**. He puts the old **one** in the wastebasket. A friend recognizes the old umbrella and returns **it**. Then the man leaves the umbrella on the train, but the conductor returns **it** the next day. The man tries very hard to throw away his umbrella, but **it** always comes back. Finally, he lends the umbrella to a friend. He never sees **it** again.

Now listen and read the conversation between Doug and Elenore.

ELENORE: Doug, where's your new sweatshirt?

DOUG: Dino has **it**. I'm wearing his sweatshirt.

ELENORE: Why?

DOUG: Sometimes Dino and I lend each other clothes.

ELENORE: But that **one** is so tight. You like baggy clothes.

DOUG: I like baggy jeans, not baggy sweatshirts. And this **one** has a hood. Hoods are in style now. And look at all these pockets. There are two big **ones** and one small **one**.

ELENORE: I'll never know what you like to wear.

GRAMMAR **PRESENTATION**
SIMPLE PRESENT TENSE AND *ONE* / *ONES* AND *IT*

	A / AN	SINGULAR COUNT NOUN		ONE
SINGULAR				
I don't need	**a**	**pen**.	I have	**one**.

	NOUN PHRASE		ONE
SINGULAR			
I don't need	**a long-sleeved shirt**.	I have	**one**.

		ADJECTIVE	SINGULAR COUNT NOUN			ADJECTIVE	ONE
SINGULAR							
Do you want	a	gray	**sweatshirt**	or	a	blue	**one**?

	ADJECTIVE	PLURAL COUNT NOUN			ADJECTIVE	ONES	
PLURAL							
The	gray	**sweatshirts**	are twenty dollars.	The	blue	**ones**	are eighteen.

THIS	ONE		THAT	ONE	
SINGULAR					
This	**one**	is my book and	that	**one**	is **Yoko's**.

	THE	+ NOUN	IT
IT			
Where's	**the**	**car**?	**It**'s on Main Street.
	POSSESSIVE ADJECTIVE + NOUN		IT
Where's	**your**	**watch**?	**It**'s on the dresser.
	THIS / THAT	+ NOUN	IT
Where's	**that**	**book**?	**It**'s on my desk.

NOTES	EXAMPLES
1. Use *one* in place of *a* or *an* plus a **singular count noun**.	**A:** Does he need a car? **B:** Yes, he needs **one**. (*one* = a car)
2. Use *one* in place of **a noun phrase**.	**A:** She doesn't want a sweatshirt with pockets. She has **one**. (*one* = a sweatshirt with pockets)
3. Use *one* or *ones* after **an adjective** in place of a singular or plural count noun.	**A:** There are three dictionaries. There are two big **ones** and a small **one**. (*ones* = dictionaries, *one* = dictionary)
4. Use *one* after **this** or **that**. ▶ **BE CAREFUL!** Do not use *ones* after **these** or **those**.	**A:** Do you need this book? **B:** No, I don't need **this one**. I need **that one**. (*one* = book) **A:** Do you want these? **B:** No, I want **those**. NOT <s>No, I want those ones.</s>
5. Use *it* in place of *the* + **a noun**.	**A:** Where is **the letter**? **B:** **It**'s on the floor. (*it* = the letter)
6. Use *it* in place of a **possessive pronoun** (*my, your, his, her, its, our,* or *their*) plus a singular count noun.	**A:** Where is **your lunch**? **B:** **It**'s in my lunch box. (*it* = my lunch)
7. Use *it* in place of **this** or **that** plus a **singular count noun**.	**A:** Where is **that cookie**? **B:** **It**'s on the floor. (*it* = that cookie)

FOCUSED PRACTICE

1 DISCOVER THE GRAMMAR

Yoko is dressing for a party. Read the conversation between Yoko and Carol.

CAROL: Hi Yoko. What's up?

YOKO: Oh, Carol. I'm going to a party. I have a nice blouse, but I need a long black skirt.

CAROL: I have <u>one</u>. Here. You can wear it.
1.

YOKO: Are you sure? It's beautiful.

CAROL: Positive. And here are two belts. Choose one.

YOKO: This <u>one</u> is nice. Is it really okay if I borrow <u>it</u> for tonight?
2.   3.

CAROL: Of course. And here's my silver necklace. <u>It</u> matches the belt.
4.

YOKO: You're right. Thanks a lot, Carol.

CAROL: No problem. Have a great time.

YOKO: Thanks.

Look at the underlined words. Circle what they refer to.

1. a. a long black skirt	**b.** a party	**c.** Yoko's skirt
2. a. skirt	**b.** belt	**c.** belts
3. a. the nice belt	**b.** a belt	**c.** a skirt
4. a. my long skirt	**b.** my silver belt	**c.** my silver necklace

2 **GETTING READY FOR COLD WEATHER**   Grammar Notes 1–7

Bertha, who lives in Florida, is planning to visit her daughter in Boston. Read the conversation between Lulu and Bertha. Replace the underlined words in the conversation. Use **one**, **ones**, *or* **it**.

LULU: Well, Bertha, are you ready for your trip? Remember, it gets pretty cold in

Boston.

BERTHA: Yes, I'm ready. I have a new coat. ~~My coat~~ is a heavy wool.
$\overset{It}{\underset{\mathbf{1.}}{}}$

LULU: Do you have a scarf?

BERTHA: Two—a white <u>scarf</u> and a red, white, and blue <u>scarf</u>. I think I need a wool hat.
      2.   3.

Do you have <u>a wool hat</u> I could borrow?
      4.

LULU: Sure. I have three wool hats. I have a red <u>wool hat</u> and two white <u>wool hats</u>.
                                                5.   6.

BERTHA: Oh, let me see the red hat.

LULU: Okay. It's in my hall closet. One minute . . . now where is <u>that hat</u>? . . .
                                                           7.

Here it is.

BERTHA: Oh, Lulu. This hat isn't for me. I look like a tomato in <u>this hat</u>.
                                                        8.

COMMUNICATION PRACTICE

3 FRUIT AND VEGETABLES

Work with a partner. Look at the pictures and complete the sentences. The first pair to label every fruit or vegetable correctly wins.

1. Rabbits eat many of these. They're long and orange. They're

   <u>c</u> <u>a</u> <u>r</u> <u>r</u> <u>o</u> <u>t</u> <u>s</u> .

2. There's an "egg" in the name of this one. It's purple. It's (a/an)

   ___ ___ ___ ___ ___ ___ ___ ___ .

3. We often put this one in a salad. It's green. It's (a/an)

   ___ ___ ___ ___ ___ ___ ___ ___ .

4. There are red ones, yellow ones, orange ones, and green ones.

   They're ___ ___ ___ ___ ___ ___ ___ .

5. Some of these are poisonous. They grow in damp places.

   They're ___ ___ ___ ___ ___ ___ ___ ___ ___ .

6. There's a saying: "You are the _____ of my eye." There's another saying: "An _____ a day keeps the doctor away." There are red ones, yellow ones, and green ones. They are

   ___ ___ ___ ___ ___ ___ .

7. This one is very sour. It's yellow. It's (a / an)

   ___ ___ ___ ___ ___ .

8. On Halloween people carve faces on this one. It's orange.

   It's (a / an) ___ ___ ___ ___ ___ ___ ___ .

9. We put these in pies. People in the United States eat these pies on Washington's birthday.

   They're ___ ___ ___ ___ ___ ___ ___ ___ .

10. This one is very watery and has a lot of seeds. It's red in the middle and green on the outside. It's (a/an)

    ___ ___ ___ ___ ___ ___ ___ ___ ___ ___ .

Now describe a fruit or vegetable. Ask the class what it is.

REVIEW OR SELFTEST

I. *Read each conversation. Circle the letter of the underlined word that is not correct.*

1. **A:** <u>Do</u> you <u>have</u> a good dictionary?
      A   B

   B: Yes, I <u>have</u>. <u>It's</u> on my desk.
           C   B

   A B C D

2. **A:** <u>Where</u> does he <u>works</u>?
         A   B

   B: He <u>works</u> at the bank <u>next to</u> the supermarket.
          C   D

   A B C D

3. **A:** <u>Does</u> he <u>need</u> a doctor?
       A   B

   B: Yes, he <u>needs</u>. He <u>has</u> a terrible earache.
           C   D

   A B C D

4. **A:** <u>Why</u> do you <u>work</u> at night?
       A   B

   B: <u>When</u> I <u>study</u> during the day.
        C   D

   A B C D

5. **A:** <u>Do</u> you <u>have</u> any sweatshirts in medium?
      A   B

   B: Yes, we <u>are</u> <u>have</u> sweatshirts in all sizes.
           C   D

   A B C D

6. **A:** Carol doesn't <u>to</u> <u>live</u> in California.
                A B

   B: <u>Where</u> does she <u>live</u>?
       C   D

   A B C D

7. **A:** <u>Who</u> <u>does</u> Carol usually <u>eats</u> lunch with?
       A   B   C

   B: She usually <u>eats</u> with Dan and Jon.
             D

   A B C D

II. *Complete the sentences. Use the present tense of the verb in parentheses.*

1. (need) _____ you _____ a suit?

2. He (wash) _____ the windows once a month.

3. Carol (have) _____ a sister and a brother.

4. Pete (be, not) _____ a lawyer.

5. Mrs. Smith (fix) _____ lamps.

6. Pete (go) _____ to the park on Tuesdays.

7. She (do) _____ the dishes every morning.

8. (speak) _____ your sister _____ English?

9. (wear) _____ the students _____ uniforms to school?

10. We (eat, not) _____ turkey for breakfast.

11. Pete often (worry) _____ about his family.

12. Who (live) _____ next to the Winstons?

13. What (make) _____ you happy?

14. What time (come) _____ your father _____ home from work?

15. Where (keep) _____ they _____ their money?

III. *Write questions. Use the simple present tense.*

1. Elenore gets up at 6:00 A.M.

   a. ___What time do you get up elenore___ ? At 6:00 A.M.

   b. ___Who gets up at 6:00 A.M.___ ? Elenore does.

   c. ___Does elenore get up at 6:00 A.M.___ ? Yes, she does.

   d. _____ ? She gets up.

2. Doug calls Noah every night at 9:00 P.M.

   a. ___Who call Noah every nigth a 900 PM___ ? Doug does.

   b. ___Who does___ ? Noah.

IV. *Complete the sentences. Use* **it**, **one**, *or* **ones**.

1. I have a green sweater and two white ___ones___ .

2. I have a green sweater. ___it___ is very warm.

3. Doug has a blue sweater and a gold ___one___ .

4. Elenore wears that jacket because ___it___ is very comfortable.

5. I like green grapes, but I don't like red ___ones___ .

6. On Thursdays, we usually watch an interesting show about animals in Australia.

   ___it___ is on channel 13 at 8:00.

7. My old watch is gold, but my new ___one___ isn't.

V. *Complete the conversations. Use* **this**, **that**, **these**, *or* **those**.

1. A: Come and meet my friend. John, ___this___ is my cousin George.

   B: Nice to meet you.

2. A: How much does the tie in your hand cost?

   B: ___this___ one costs thirty-five dollars. It's silk. But ___those___ ties on the

   other side of the room only cost ten dollars.

   A: Thanks.

3. A: Who's ___that___ boy across the street?

   B: It's Alex.

4. A: You are a very good photographer. ___these___ photos are excellent.

   B: Thank you. I have some more in my bag.

   A: Please show them to me.

   B: Okay.

   A: They're wonderful. What about ___those___ photos on the wall? Are they your

   photos, too?

   B: Yes, they are.

   A: Wow! You're really talented!

VI. *Correct these sentences.*

1. Doug ~~like~~ likes soccer.

2. She ~~isn't~~ doesn't write a letter every week.

3. Does Carol ~~needs~~ need an umbrella?

4. ~~This is~~ these are my gloves.

5. Do they ~~wants~~ any eggs?

6. Norma ~~is~~ teaches Spanish.

7. Who does cooks in your house?

8. This are my friends.

9. Those magazine has wonderful photos.

10. Does Doug likes basketball?

▶ *To check your answers, go to the Answer Key on page 146.*

FROM GRAMMAR TO WRITING
TIME WORD CONNECTORS:
FIRST, NEXT, AFTER THAT, THEN, FINALLY

 Which paragraph sounds better, Paragraph A or B? Why?

Paragraph A

I like to watch my roommate prepare tea. She boils water and pours the boiling water in a cup with a teabag in it. She removes the tea bag and adds sugar. She adds lemon. She adds ice. She sips the tea and says, "Mmm. This tea is just the way I like it."

Paragraph B

I like to watch my roommate prepare tea. First, she boils some water and pours the boiling water in a cup with a teabag in it. Next, she removes the teabag and adds some sugar. After that, she adds some lemon. Then she adds some ice. Finally, she sips the tea and says, "Mmm. This tea is just the way I like it."

Study this information about time word connectors.

Time Word Connectors

You can make your writing clearer by using **time word connectors**. They show the order that things happen. Some common ones are: **first**, **next**, **after that**, **then**, and **finally**.

Note the use of the **comma** after these words.

- **First**, you add the water. **Next**, you add the sugar.

2 *Use time word connectors to show the order of things in this paragraph.*

I take a shower. I have breakfast. I drive to the train station. I take a train and a bus. I get to work.

Now write a paragraph about a routine you follow. Use time word connectors. Here are some ideas:

a. Every Saturday morning . . .

b. Every New Year's Day . . .

c. Every year on my birthday . . .

REVIEW OR SELFTEST
ANSWER KEY

I.
1. C   3. C   5. C   7. C
2. B   4. C   6. A

IV.
1. ones   4. it   6. It
2. It   5. ones   7. one
3. one

II.
1. Do, need
2. washes
3. has
4. isn't ('s not) (is not)
5. fixes
6. goes
7. does
8. Does, speak
9. Do, wear
10. don't eat
11. worries
12. lives
13. makes
14. does, come
15. do, keep

V.
1. this   3. that
2. This / those   4. These / those

III.
1. a. When does Elenore get up? (What time does Elenore get up?)
   b. Who gets up at 6:00 A.M.?
   c. Does Elenore get up at 6:00 A.M.?
   d. What does Elenore do at 6:00 A.M.?
2. a. Who calls Noah every night at 9:00 P.M.?
   b. Who does Doug call every night at 9:00 P.M.?

VI.
2. She <u>doesn't</u> write a letter every week.
3. Does Carol <u>need</u> an umbrella?
4. This is my <u>glove</u>. (<u>These are</u> my gloves.)
5. Do they <u>want</u> any eggs?
6. Norma teaches Spanish.
7. Who cooks in your house?
8. <u>These are</u> my friends. (<u>This is</u> my friend.)
9. Those magazines <u>have</u> wonderful photos. (<u>That magazine</u> has wonderful photos.)
10. Does Doug <u>like</u> basketball?

Answers to Exercise 7 on page 121

1. Is; Yes, it is.
2. Does; No, it doesn't.
3. Does; Yes, it does.
4. Does; Yes, it does.
5. Is; Yes, it is.
6. Do; Yes, they do.
7. Is; Yes, it is.
8. Does; No, it doesn't.
9. Do; Yes, they do.
10. Is; Yes, it is.
11. Is; No, it isn't.
12. Are; Yes, they are.

Answers to Exercise 7 on page 130

1. b   4. b
2. c   5. a
3. b   6. c

Student B, complete sentences 5–8. Then listen to your partner read sentences 1–4. Say "That's right" or correct your partner's sentence. Then read sentences 5–8 to your partner. Your partner says "That's right" or corrects your sentence.

1. People in Japan don't wear shoes in their home. When they enter a home, they remove their shoes and put on slippers.

2. People in Korea eat rice cake soup on New Year's Day. Children often wear red jackets with sleeves of many colors.

3. People in Thailand bow to show respect. Younger people usually bow first.

4. In Brazil during Carnival people wear strange and beautiful costumes. Brazilians don't work during Carnival. They dance in the streets.

5. In Saudi Arabia at the time of Ramadan, Moslems _____ or
   _____ during daylight. Ramadan _____ for thirty days. At
     b. (drink / don't drink)   c. (lasts / doesn't last)
               a. (eat / don't eat)
   the end of Ramadan there _____ a three-day celebration.
                            d. (is / isn't)

6. On New Year's Day, Chinese children _____ money in red envelopes from
                         a. (receive / don't receive)
   their parents and grandparents.

7. In the United States, people usually _____ on July 4th. They
                         a. (work / don't work)
   _____ fireworks and _____ barbecues.
     b. (watch / don't watch)   c. (have / don't have)

8. In Denmark, people _____ on their friends' doors and
              a. (bang / don't bang)
   _____ fireworks on New Year's Eve.
     b. (set off / don't set off)

Now work with your partner. Write about customs you know well. Read your sentences to the class.

_____

_____

_____

_____

THE SIMPLE PAST TENSE

PREVIEW

Carol is visiting San Francisco. She is talking on the phone to her mother, Elenore, in New York. Listen and read their conversation.

THE WINSTONS' THANKSGIVING DAY

CAROL: Hi, Mom.

ELENORE: Hi, Carol. Gee, we really missed you for Thanksgiving.

CAROL: I missed you, too.

ELENORE: How's San Francisco? When did you and Yoko arrive?

CAROL: We arrived late Wednesday night. San Francisco's great. On Thanksgiving Day we took a sight-seeing bus all around the city. Then we rode on a cable car and walked around Fisherman's Wharf. We ate fish at a restaurant there and had a great time. What about you and Dad? Did you have a nice Thanksgiving?

ELENORE: Well, Uncle Bob and Aunt Valerie invited us for dinner.

148

CAROL: How was it?

ELENORE: Dinner was delicious. Aunt Valerie made a huge turkey. I brought cranberry sauce, Norma baked a pumpkin pie, and Dad prepared pumpkin curry soup.

CAROL: Pumpkin curry soup? That's different. How did it taste?

ELENORE: I liked it, but Uncle Bob didn't like it at all. He tried one spoonful and shouted, "Fire!" Then he drank four glasses of water.

CAROL: Poor Uncle Bob!

ELENORE: Poor Dad! After dinner Uncle Bob turned on the TV and watched a football game. You know how Dad hates football.

CAROL: Did you stay long?

ELENORE: No, we left early.

CAROL: Well, that was a good idea. Remember last summer when we went to Massachusetts with Aunt Valerie and Uncle Bob? Uncle Bob and Dad had that big fight.

ELENORE: Please, Carol, don't remind me. Well, I hope you and Yoko enjoy the rest of your vacation.

CAROL: Thanks, Mom. I'll call you next week. Bye.

ELENORE: Bye.

COMPREHENSION CHECK

Check (✔) who did what activity.

	Carol	Carol's parents	No one
1. visited San Francisco	❏	❏	❏
2. visited Aunt Valerie and Uncle Bob	❏	❏	❏
3. went to Massachusetts last summer	❏	❏	❏
4. saw a fire	❏	❏	❏
5. rode on a cable car	❏	❏	❏
6. ate turkey, cranberry sauce, and pumpkin pie	❏	❏	❏

WITH A PARTNER

Practice the conversation on pages 148 and 149.

SIMPLE PAST TENSE: REGULAR VERBS—AFFIRMATIVE AND NEGATIVE STATEMENTS

GRAMMAR **IN CONTEXT**

WARM UP   Look at the chart. Were you in any of these cities?
What cities? When?

> ### The World's Ten Largest Cities
>
> **Seoul, South Korea**
> **São Paulo, Brazil**
> **Bombay (Mumbai), India**
> **Jakarta, Indonesia**
> **Moscow, Russia**
> **Istanbul, Turkey**
> **Mexico City, Mexico**
> **Shanghai, China**
> **Tokyo, Japan**
> **New York City, United States**

Source:
infoplease.com, 1997

Listen and read the following postcard.

Hi Elenore and Pete,

   Ali and I are having a great time here in
this magical city.

   Last night we **walked** along the Seine River.
Today we **dined** in Montmartre and we **visited**
the Louvre. (I **didn't** really **like** the Mona Lisa,
but maybe I **didn't understand** it.)

   We're now at the Eiffel Tower and it looks
just like it does in the photos.

   Hope all is well with you.

                    Love,
                    Wendy and Ali

France

To:

Mr. and Mrs. Pete Winston
345 West 76th Street
New York, New York 10023
U.S.A.

What city did Wendy and Ali visit?

GRAMMAR **PRESENTATION**
SIMPLE PAST TENSE: REGULAR VERBS—
AFFIRMATIVE AND NEGATIVE STATEMENTS

AFFIRMATIVE STATEMENTS	
SUBJECT	**BASE FORM OF VERB + -ED, -D, IED**
I You He She It We You They	cook**ed**. arrive**d**. cr**ied**.

NEGATIVE STATEMENTS		
SUBJECT	*DID NOT*	**BASE FORM OF VERB**
I You He She It We You They	**did not didn't**	**cook**. **arrive**. **cry**.

SOME COMMON PAST TIME MARKERS		
YESTERDAY	*AGO*	*LAST*
yesterday morning **yesterday** afternoon **yesterday** evening	two days **ago** a week **ago** a month **ago** a year **ago**	**last** night **last** Monday **last** week **last** summer

NOTES	EXAMPLES
1. Use the **simple past tense** to talk about an event that happened in the past. Past ◄———X——— Now ——————► Future *I arrived last night.*	• I **arrived** last night.
2. There are three endings for the regular simple past tense: *-d, -ed, -ied*.	• I bake**d** a cake. • We cook**ed** spaghetti. • They stud**ied** Japanese.
3. In the past tense, the verb form is the same for all persons.	• **I visited** my sister last night. • **She visited** me this morning. • **We visited** our aunt this afternoon.
4. For negative statements in the past, use ***did not* + the base form of the verb**. Use the contraction ***didn't*** for negative statements in speaking or informal writing.	• We **did not stay** at a hotel. • He **did not like** the painting. • We **didn't stay** at a hotel.
5. **Time markers** usually come at the beginning or at the end of a sentence.	• **Yesterday morning** I studied. • I studied **yesterday morning**.
6. ***Today*, *this morning*, *this afternoon*,** and ***this evening*** can be past time markers if they mean "before now."	• I studied grammar **today**. (It is now 9:00 P.M. I studied grammar in the afternoon.) • **This morning** I listened to the news. (It is now afternoon.)

> **REFERENCE NOTE**
> See Appendix 15, page A-15, for complete spelling and pronunciation rules for the simple past tense.

FOCUSED PRACTICE

1 DISCOVER THE GRAMMAR

Read these sentences and underline the past-tense verbs. Then write the base form (dictionary form) of the verb next to each sentence. Circle the four other time markers.

1. (Yesterday) we <u>walked</u> around Fisherman's Wharf. _____ walk _____

2. We <u>arrived</u> (last Wednesday night.) _arrive_

3. Uncle Bob and Aunt Valerie <u>invited</u> us to their house. _invite_

4. Norma <u>baked</u> a pie (this morning.) _bake_

5. Aunt Valerie <u>cooked</u> a huge turkey. _cook_

6. The bus <u>stopped</u> at the corner (a few minutes ago.) _stop_

7. We <u>studied</u> history (last night.) _studi_

2 SPELLING AND PRONUNCIATION   Grammar Notes 2–3

Complete the sentences. Use the past tense of the verbs in the box. See Appendix 15 on page A-15 for spelling rules for the regular simple past tense.

watch	visit	cook	arrive	walk	study	bake	joke	want	hug

	/t/	/d/	/ɪd/
1. I'm sorry I'm late. I ___missed___ my train.	✔	☐	☐
2. The plane _____ on time.	☐	☐	☐
3. Last night she _____ her uncle in the hospital.	☐	☐	☐
4. He _____ hot cereal yesterday morning.	☐	☐	☐
5. I'm tired. Yesterday I _____ up a lot of hills in San Francisco.	☐	☐	☐
6. Last year she _____ to live in the city, but now she likes the country.	☐	☐	☐
7. We _____ at the library this afternoon.	☐	☐	☐
8. Last night I _____ a good movie on TV.	☐	☐	☐
9. Uncle Bob _____ about Dad's pumpkin curry soup.	☐	☐	☐
10. Everybody _____ and kissed me at my graduation.	☐	☐	☐

▭ *Now listen to the sentences. Then listen again and check (✔) the final sound of each verb. See Appendix 15 on page A-15 for pronunciation rules for the regular simple past tense.*

3 **A POSTCARD FROM SAN FRANCISCO**

Carol sent her grandmother a postcard from San Francisco. Complete the sentences. Use the simple past tense of each verb.

The Golden Gate Bridge   Chinatown

San Francisco Sights

Fisherman's Wharf   Cable Car

Sunday

Dear Grandma Lulu,

   Greetings from San Francisco! Yoko and I ____rented____ a car last
                                                    1. (rent)

Wednesday morning in Oregon. We _____ in San Francisco
                                          2. (arrive)

Wednesday night. We love it here. It's a very modern and open city.

Thursday we _____ Fisherman's Wharf and Chinatown. Friday
                     3. (visit)

we _____ around Berkeley with Yoko's friends. Yoko's uncle
        4. (walk)

_____ us to his home in Oakland, but we _____ to
     5. (invite)   6. (want, not)

drive anymore, so we _____ him. We _____ our
                            7. (visit, not)   8. (pack)

bags this morning and we're on our way home.

   All my books are at school, so I can't study, but traveling is an

education, isn't it?

   I hope you had a nice Thanksgiving.   Love,
                                                    Carol

USA 34

To: *Mrs. Lulu Winston*
6103 Collins Ave.
Miami Beach, FL 33130

④ GETTING AROUND
Grammar Note 5

Complete the conversations. Use **last**, **ago**, *or* **yesterday**.

1.   **PETE:** Hi, Bob. How are you doing?

         BOB: Fine.

      PETE: Were you away?

        BOB: Yes. I attended a conference in Washington _____ week.
                                                      a.

      PETE: Oh, lucky you. Washington's beautiful this time of year. I was there a couple

               of months _____ and the weather was awful. When did you get
                                   b.

               back to New York?

        BOB: _____ .
                   c.

2. **ELENORE:** Pete, where are the Strams?

      PETE: In Prague. They arrived there _____ morning.
                                        a.

  ELENORE: Wow! _____ month they were in Brazil. And a year
                             b.

               _____ they were in Bangkok. They really get around.
                 c.

⑤ THE WINSTONS' THANKSGIVING
Grammar Notes 1–6

Read the conversations on pages 148 and 149 again. Write affirmative or negative past-tense sentences.

1. Carol and Yoko / visit / San Francisco / last week

    Carol and Yoko visited San Francisco last week.

2. Carol and Yoko / visit / Boston / last week

    Carol and Yoko didn't visit Boston last week.

3. Uncle Bob / watch / a football game / on Thanksgiving

    _____

4. Carol / watch / a football game / on Thanksgiving

    _____

5. Aunt Valerie / cook / a huge turkey / last Thursday

    _____

6. Carol and Yoko / cook / a turkey / on Thanksgiving

    _____

6 WRONG MESSAGES

Grammar Notes 1–3, 5–6

Listen to Pete and Elenore's phone messages. Then read this conversation between Elenore and Pete. Correct Pete's three mistakes.

PETE: Hello.

ELENORE: Hi Pete. Listen. I'm at the hairdresser's. I'll be home at about 6:30.

PETE: Okay. Thanks for calling.

ELENORE: Any messages?

PETE: Well, a James Mills called. He and Joe arrived today. They're at the Central Hotel.

ELENORE: Okay. Any other messages?

PETE: Yes. Doug. He invited Noah for dinner.

ELENORE: Oh that's nice. I'm glad I cooked a lot this morning. Well, see you in about an hour.

PETE: Okay. Bye.

7 EDITING

Find and correct the three mistakes in this postcard.

Dear Elenore and Pete,

They say everyone loves Rio. Now we know why.

Yesterday morning we did watch a soccer game on Ipanema Beach. Then we visit Sugarloaf. In the evening we're enjoying a huge and delicious meal at a churrascaria.

The people are friendly and the weather is great. Regards to Norma, Carol, and Doug.

Love,

Dahlia and Josh

Brazil

To:
Mr. and Mrs. Pete Winston
345 West 76th Street
New York, New York 10023
U.S.A.

COMMUNICATION PRACTICE

8 WHAT I DID LAST WEEKEND

Work in small groups. Check (✔) the activities you did last weekend. Then tell
your group more about them.

_____ **1.** I watched TV.

_____ **2.** I listened to music.

_____ **3.** I visited friends or relatives.

_____ **4.** I talked on the
telephone.

_____ **5.** I played a sport.

_____ **6.** I worked.

_____ **7.** I studied.

EXAMPLE:

I watched TV Friday night. I watched Hitchcock's movie *The Birds*. It was scary.

9 TALKING ABOUT FEELINGS

Work in small groups. Write five sentences that begin, **"I feel bad. I didn't . . ."**
Then write five sentences that begin, **"I'm a little angry. My friend didn't . . ."**
Use the verbs in the box or add your own.

| call | visit | talk to | wash | answer | help | thank | clean | return | study |

EXAMPLES:

1. I feel bad. I didn't thank Maria for the gift.

2. I'm a little angry. My friend didn't return my sweater. She borrowed it
a month ago.

Now read a sentence to your group. Your classmates listen and respond.

10 GUESS THE SITUATION

Work in small groups. Read the sentences. Who is speaking? What happened?
Discuss your answers with your group. Use the verbs in the box.

| delivered | arrived | died | played | dialed | graduated |

EXAMPLE:

"I'm so sorry. Our baby-sitter missed her bus and arrived thirty minutes late."

A woman is speaking. The woman and her husband arrived late at a party.

1. "Thanks. I enjoyed the game. Let's meet next week."

2. "The pizza smells good. Here's twenty dollars, and keep the change."

3. "Congratulations."

4. "Sorry, wrong number."

5. "I'm so sorry to hear about your grandfather's death."

SIMPLE PAST TENSE: IRREGULAR VERBS—AFFIRMATIVE AND NEGATIVE STATEMENTS

GRAMMAR **IN CONTEXT**

WARM UP   What does, "You never know what will happen" mean to you?

🎞 *Listen and read this Chinese folktale.*

YOU NEVER KNOW WHAT WILL HAPPEN

A long time ago there lived a poor Chinese peasant. One day a beautiful horse appeared. When the peasant's friends **saw** the horse, they **said**, "How lucky you are!"

The peasant answered, "You never know what will happen."

After two days, the horse **ran** away. The peasant's friends **came** and **said**, "What a terrible thing. How unlucky you are! The fine horse ran away." The peasant **didn't get** excited. He simply said, "You never know what will happen."

Exactly one week later the horse returned. And it **brought** three other horses. When the peasant's friends **saw** the horses, they **said** to their friend, "Oh. You are so lucky. Now you have four horses to help you." The peasant looked at them and once again **said**, "You never know what will happen."

The next morning the peasant's oldest son **was** in the field. Suddenly one of the horses **ran** into him, and the boy **fell** to the ground.

He **was** badly hurt. He **lost** the use of his leg. Indeed, this **was** terrible, and many people **came** to the peasant and expressed their sadness for his son's misfortune. But again the peasant simply **said**, "You never know what will happen."

A month after the son's accident, soldiers **rode** into the village. They shouted, "There are problems along the border. We are taking every healthy young man to fight." The soldiers **took** every other young man, but they **didn't take** the peasant's son. Every other young man **fought** in the border war, and every man died. But the peasant's son lived a long and happy life. As his father **said**, you never know what will happen.

GRAMMAR **PRESENTATION**
SIMPLE PAST TENSE: IRREGULAR VERBS— AFFIRMATIVE AND NEGATIVE STATEMENTS

AFFIRMATIVE STATEMENTS		
SUBJECT	**VERB**	
I You He She It We You They	**saw**	the horses.

NEGATIVE STATEMENTS			
SUBJECT	**DID NOT / DIDN'T**	**BASE FORM OF VERB**	
I You He She It We You They	**did not** **didn't**	see	the soldiers.

NOTES

1. **Irregular past tense verbs** do not add *-ed* in affirmative sentences. They have different forms.

2. For **negative statements** in the past, use *did not* + **the base form of the verb**. (except for the verb *be*)

3. The past tense of *be* is *was* or *were*. The negative of *was* is *was not*, and the negative of *were* is *were not*. The contractions of *was not* and *were not* are *wasn't* and *weren't*.

EXAMPLES

- We **saw** a beautiful horse.
- The horse **ran** home.
- She **came** late.
- He **brought** a friend to school.
- He **ate** a huge lunch.

- They **did not visit** Los Angeles.
- She **did not eat** lunch.

- I **was** at the library last night.
- They **were not** home this morning.
- It **wasn't** late.
- They **weren't** in Tokyo.

> **REFERENCE NOTE**
> See Appendix 12, page A-13, for a list of irregular past tense verb forms.

FOCUSED PRACTICE

1 DISCOVER THE GRAMMAR

Read this story that Al Brown told his students. Underline all the past tense verbs. Circle the irregular verbs.

Bon Appétit!

Many years ago my grandfather, Benjamin Brown, (took) a cruise on the Mediterranean Sea. The first evening at dinner a Frenchman sat down next to my grandfather. Before he sat down, the Frenchman looked at my grandfather and said, "Bon appetit."

My grandfather stood up and said, "Ben Brown." The same thing happened the next evening and the one after that. My grandfather said to an Englishman on the ship, "I don't understand my dinner partner. Every evening he comes to dinner and introduces himself." The Englishman, who spoke French, asked my grandfather some more questions. Soon he understood my grandfather's mistake. He explained to my grandfather that "bon appetit" was not the man's name, but was French for "Enjoy your meal."

The next night my grandfather came to dinner after the Frenchman. My grandfather smiled and with a perfect French accent said, "Bon appetit." The Frenchman stood up and replied, "Ben Brown."

2 CAROL AND YOKO IN SAN FRANCISCO   Grammar Notes 1–2

Study these irregular verbs.

Base form	Past form
do	did
drive	drove
eat	ate
feel	felt
find	found
go	went
leave	left
meet	met
send	sent

(continued on next page)

Now complete the sentences. Use the verbs in the box on page 161.

1. Carol and Yoko (not) ___didn't eat___ turkey on Thanksgiving. They ___ate___ fish.

2. Carol _____ Yoko's friends from Berkeley for the first time last Wednesday.

3. Lucky Yoko! She _____ twenty dollars on a cable car in San Francisco.

4. Carol didn't get to San Francisco by bus. She rented a car and _____ there with Yoko.

5. Yoko (not) _____ her homework on Thursday or Friday. She _____ it on Saturday and Sunday.

6. After their trip to San Francisco, Yoko and Carol _____ very relaxed.

7. Carol and Yoko (not) _____ to a concert. They _____ to the movies.

8. Carol _____ a postcard to her grandmother.

9. Yoko and Carol _____ San Francisco at noon on Sunday. They arrived home at nine o'clock Sunday night.

3 THANKSGIVING VACATION

Study these irregular verbs. Now complete the conversation. Use the verbs in the box.

Base form	Past form
forget	forgot
have	had
hide	hid
read	read (pronounced /rɛd/)
sleep	slept
speak	spoke
steal	stole
swim	swam

AL BROWN: Welcome back. I hope you all enjoyed your Thanksgiving vacation.

YOLANDA: Oh, I _____had_____ a great time. I visited Los Angeles for four days.
  1.

  I _____ in a pool and played tennis every day.
    2.

AL BROWN: What about you, Maria?

MARIA: On my vacation I _____ late every day, and I _____
    3.   4.

  two novels.

AL BROWN: In English?

MARIA: No, in Spanish.

AL BROWN: Oh, well. Yuriko, did you have a nice vacation?

YURIKO: Yes, I did. My boyfriend called me yesterday. We _____ for over
    5.

  an hour.

AL BROWN: Bekir, why are you so sad?

BEKIR: I want to forget my vacation. Last Friday I _____ to lock my door
    6.

  and someone _____ my TV.
    7.

AL BROWN: Did the thief take any money?

BEKIR: No. I _____ my money in my grammar book.
    8.

  The thief didn't look there.

COMMUNICATION PRACTICE

4 A MEMORY GAME

Play a memory game with the class. Sit in a circle. The first student tells one thing he or she did yesterday. The next student tells what the first student did and then what he or she did. Continue as long as each student remembers what the others have already said.

EXAMPLE:

A: I went to the movies.

B: A went to the movies, and I read a novel.

5 HOW WAS YOUR DAY?

Work in small groups. Tell about a wonderful day and a terrible day. Use **First,** **Then,** *and* **After that.**

EXAMPLES:

I had a wonderful day today.

First, I saw my grandmother.

Then, I went to the park.

After that, I rented a video.

Yesterday I had a terrible day.

First, I got to school late.

Then, I broke my glasses.

After that, someone stole my wallet.

6 A SPECIAL PERSON

Complete the story. Use your imagination. Read your story to your classmates. Listen to their stories.

_____ ago I met a _____. He / She had _____

and _____. He / She came from _____. We spoke about

_____ and _____. I said, "_____." He / She said,

"_____." Then he/she left. I felt _____.

7 SURPRISES

Work in small groups. Sometimes you don't know what will happen. Tell your group a story from your life with a surprising ending. Then tell the class one of your group's stories.

EXAMPLE:

As a child, Bob hated school. He never did well in school. His sisters and brothers always brought home prizes for their excellent schoolwork, but not Bob. Bob's parents worried about him. But in his second year of high school Bob had a wonderful chemistry teacher. He became interested in chemistry. From that time on he studied hard. He is now a well-known chemistry professor at a top university.

SIMPLE PAST TENSE: *YES / NO* AND *WH-* QUESTIONS

GRAMMAR **IN CONTEXT**

WARM UP   Do you have anything (a watch, a ring, a necklace) that belonged to an older relative? What is it? Who did it belong to?

EXAMPLE:
I have a beautiful old watch. It belonged to my grandfather's brother. When he died, my grandfather gave it to me.

Look at these questions. Listen and read the conversation on page 166. Then answer the questions.

1. **What did** Norma **lose**?
   a. a boyfriend   **b.** a watch   **c.** a ring

2. **Who did** it **belong** to?
   a. her great-   **b.** her best friend   **c.** her father
      grandmother

3. **When did** she **get** it?
   a. many years ago   **b.** a few years ago   **c.** a few days ago

4. **Who called** her?
   a. the new   **b.** her great-   **c.** her friend
      math teacher   grandmother

5. **Did** Norma **get** it back?
   a. No, she didn't.   **b.** Yes, she did.   **c.** It doesn't say.

ALICE: **What happened**, Norma? You look like you lost your best friend.

NORMA: Well, I'm pretty upset. I lost my ring.

ALICE: Oh, that's awful. Was it valuable?

NORMA: Not really. But it was valuable to me. It belonged to my great-grandmother. My mom gave it to me just a few days ago, at Thanksgiving.

ALICE: **Where did** you **lose** it?

NORMA: I'm not sure. Maybe I lost it in the parking lot. The ring was loose.

ALICE: **When did** you last **have** the ring?

NORMA: Well, I know I had it this morning.

[Norma's cell phone rings.]

NORMA: Hello?

MARY: Hello. I'm Mary Connelly. Is this Norma Winston?

NORMA: Yes?

MARY: I'm the new math teacher at Kennedy High School. I found a ring in the teacher's lunchroom. **Did** you, by any chance, **leave** a ring there?

NORMA: Yes, I did. **How did** you **know** it was my ring?

MARY: I found the ring and I asked around. Elaine Brown remembered the ring on your finger.

NORMA: Oh that's wonderful. I'm glad Elaine has a good eye for jewelry.

MARY: Anyway, don't worry. Your ring is safe.

NORMA: Thanks so much. And welcome to Kennedy.

MARY: Thanks. See you tomorrow.

GRAMMAR **PRESENTATION**
SIMPLE PAST TENSE: *YES / NO* QUESTIONS AND SHORT ANSWERS AND *WH-* QUESTIONS

YES / NO QUESTIONS		
DID	**SUBJECT**	**BASE FORM OF VERB**
Did	I you he she it we you they	**work**? **eat**?

SHORT ANSWERS					
AFFIRMATIVE			**NEGATIVE**		
Yes,	you I he she it you we they	**did**.	**No**,	you I he she it you we they	**didn't**.

WH- QUESTIONS ABOUT THE SUBJECT	
WH- **WORD**	**PAST-TENSE VERB**
Who	**called**?
What	**happened**?

ANSWERS
Norma did. (Norma called.)
She lost her ring.

OTHER *WH-* QUESTIONS			
WH- **WORD**	***DID***	**SUBJECT**	**BASE FORM OF VERB**
What		I	**forget**?
Where		you	**go**?
When	**did**	he	**arrive**?
Why		we	**leave**?
Who(m)		you	**call**?
How long		they	**stay**?

ANSWERS
You forgot your book.
I went to San Francisco.
Before lunch.
We didn't want to be late.
The teacher.
A few hours. For a few hours.

NOTES	**EXAMPLES**

1. *Yes / No* **questions** in the past tense have the same form for regular and irregular verbs except for the verb *be*.

regular verb
• **Did** you **enjoy** the movie?

irregular verb
• **Did** you **write** the letter?

• **Were** you at work yesterday?

---

2. Most *wh-* **questions** in the past begin with the question word followed by ***did* + the subject + the base form** of the verb.

• **Where did** Bill **study**?
• **Who did** Bill **study** with?
• **Why did** Bill **study** there?
• **What did** Bill **study**?

Wh- questions in the past do not use *did* when the question is about the subject.

subject
• Bill studied in the library with Jon.
   A: Who studied? Bill did.
   NOT ~~Who did study?~~

subject
• The glass broke.
   A: What broke? The glass did.
   NOT ~~What did break?~~

Wh- questions in the past with *be* do not use *did*.

A: Where were you last night?
B: I was in the library.

---

3. Questions that begin with *How* ask about the manner in which something occurred.

A: How did you **get** to school?
B: By bus.

Questions that begin with *How long* ask for the length of time. We often use *for* in the answer.

A: How long did you **stay**?
B: For two hours. (We stayed for two hours.)

Note the form for a question about how long something took.

A: How long did it take you to get there?
B: An hour.

4. We usually give short answers to *yes / no* and *wh-* questions, but we can also give long answers.

> **A:** Did you work yesterday afternoon?
> **B:** **Uh-huh.**
> **B:** **Yes.**
> **B:** **Yes, I did.**
> **B:** **Yes, I worked yesterday afternoon.**
>
> **A:** Where did you go?
> **B:** **To the park.**
> **B:** **We went to the park.**

PRONUNCIATION NOTE

Yes / no questions use rising intonation. *Wh-* questions use falling intonation.

(Did you hear the story? What did you think about it?)

REFERENCE NOTE

For more notes about *wh-* questions, see Part III and Unit 30.

FOCUSED PRACTICE

① DISCOVER THE GRAMMAR

First read these questions and write the letter of the two possible answers to each question. Then read the story and circle the correct answer.

a. Yes, he did.	f. A blanket.
b. Paul's mother.	g. Because he wanted to remember his grandfather.
c. Paul lost it.	h. No, he didn't.
d. It tore.	i. A change purse.
e. Paul's son.	j. Because his parents worked.

1. What happened to the change purse? _____c_____ or _____d_____

2. What happened to the pencil case? _____ or _____

3. Did Paul's grandfather **play** with him? _____ or _____

4. Did Paul **play** with his grandmother? _____ or _____

5. What did Paul's grandfather **give** him? _____ or _____

6. What did Paul **make** the pencil case into? _____ or _____

7. Who made the book bag into a pencil case? _____ or _____

8. Who found Paul's story? _____ or _____

9. Why did Paul **spend** a lot of time at his grandparents' house? _____ or _____

10. Why did Paul **write** about his grandfather's blanket? _____ or _____

GRANDPA'S BLANKET

As a young child, I was quiet and shy. I was also sick a lot of the time. My parents worked, and I spent a lot of time at my grandparents' house. While my grandmother cleaned and cooked, my grandfather played with me.

I was six when my grandfather died. A few months before he died, he gave me a beautiful blue and white blanket. I loved the blanket very much because it reminded me of my grandfather. But after a couple of years, the blanket didn't look very good. It had holes and stains. I didn't want to throw the

blanket away, so my mother made the blanket into a book bag. I was proud of the book bag, and I used it to carry my books to school every day for a couple of years. Then the book bag tore. I begged my mother to make something out of it. She made it into a pencil case. After a few months, the pencil case tore too. By then I could sew, and I made the pencil case into a small change purse.

I used it for three years, but one day I lost it. I felt bad. My friends and family said, "Forget about it, Paul. You can't make something out of nothing."

I thought about it for a while. I decided my friends and family were wrong. There *was* a way to make something out of nothing. I wrote down the story of my grandfather's blanket. Last week my son found my story in our attic. My son asked me about the blanket. And he asked about my grandfather. Grandpa and his blanket aren't gone.

Grandpa's Blanket

---

② JUAN'S GRANDFATHER   Grammar Notes 1–4

Juan told the class a family story about his grandfather. Write questions about the story. Then listen to the story and answer the questions.

1. Where / this story take place?

   Where does this story take place? _____? In ___Senegal.___

2. Juan's grandfather / have / an interpreter?

   _____? _____

3. Juan's grandfather / like / his interpreter?

   _____? Yes, _____

4. How long / it take / the interpreter to tell a joke?

   _____? Ten _____

5. What / the interpreter / say to the crowd?

   _____? He said, "_____"

3 BEKIR'S GRANDPARENTS

Ali asked Bekir questions about his grandparents. Write questions to complete their conversation. Use the words in parentheses.

ALI: As a child, <u>did you live with your grandparents</u>?
1. (did / live / with your grandparents)

BEKIR: No. My mother's parents lived next door. My father's parents lived far away.

ALI: _____?
2. (Where / your father's parents / live)

BEKIR: In the south of Turkey.

ALI: _____?
3. (What / your grandfather / do)

BEKIR: He had a farm.

ALI: _____?
4. (work / long hours)

BEKIR: Oh yes. He worked more than twelve hours a day.

ALI: _____?
5. (have / a large farm)

BEKIR: Yes. It belonged to his father before him.

ALI: _____?
6. (What / your grandmother / do)

BEKIR: She helped my grandfather with the farm. She worked hard, too. She brought up

my father and his seven sisters and brothers.

ALI: _____?
7. (Where / your grandparents / meet)

BEKIR: Their parents arranged their marriage.

ALI: _____?
8. (When / they / meet)

BEKIR: In the 1940s.

ALI: _____?
9. (have / a happy marriage)

BEKIR: I think so. They never complained.

ALI: Are your grandparents alive today?

BEKIR: My grandfather died six years ago, but my grandmother is still alive. She lives with

my father's older brother on the farm.

4 THE HISTORY OF THANKSGIVING
Grammar Notes 2–3

Read about Thanksgiving in the United States. Then write questions that the underlined words answer.

<u>In 1620</u> a group of people came to America from England. They were the Pilgrims.
   1.
They left England <u>because the king of England didn't allow them to practice their religion</u>.
                                                2.
   <u>The Pilgrims</u> wanted to sail to Virginia and join the first English settlers. But their boat
   3.
landed to the north, in Massachusetts.

   Massachusetts has a cold climate, and the Pilgrims had a difficult time. But with the

help of friendly Native Americans, they learned <u>to hunt and grow crops for food</u>.
                                                      4.
   After a difficult year, the Pilgrims gathered their first harvest. They celebrated with a

big feast. They invited <u>the Native Americans</u> to this feast. The feast lasted <u>for three days</u>.
                              5.   6.

1. When _did the Pilgrims come to America?_

2. Why _____

3. Who _____

4. What _____

5. Who(m) _____

6. How long _____

⑤ EDITING

Read the conversation between Eun Young and a classmate. There are six mistakes. The first one has been corrected. Find and correct the other five.

EUN YOUNG: Ch' suk is in some ways like the American Thanksgiving. It's the harvest moon festival. We celebrated it about three months ago.

CLASSMATE: Did you ~~enjoyed~~ ^enjoy^ it?

EUN YOUNG: Not this year. This year I was here in Oregon, but last year I celebrated it with my family and it was great.

CLASSMATE: What you did last year?

EUN YOUNG: I went to my hometown, Pusan. As usual, traffic was awful.

CLASSMATE: Oh yeah? How long did the trip took?

EUN YOUNG: It usually takes three hours, but it took six hours. Everyone travels on this holiday.

CLASSMATE: Why you did go there?

EUN YOUNG: My grandparents live there. I always visit them on Ch' suk.

CLASSMATE: What did you there?

EUN YOUNG: My cousins and I played games, exchanged gifts, and ate mooncakes. We also visited the graves of our ancestors.

CLASSMATE: Did you missed it this year?

EUN YOUNG: I certainly did.

COMMUNICATION PRACTICE

6 A WONDERFUL VACATION

Write questions about a wonderful vacation. Answer your questions. Then ask your partner about his or her vacation.

VACATION	YOU	YOUR PARTNER
Where / go		
Why / go there		
go there / alone		
Who / go with		
Where / stay		
How long / stay		
How / get there		
What / do		
buy / special souvenirs		
eat / special food		
meet / interesting people		
take / good photos		

EXAMPLE:
A: Where did you go?
B: I went to Hawaii.
A: Did you go there alone?
B: No, I went there with two friends.

Now tell the class about your partner's vacation.

7 MY GRANDPARENTS

Work with a partner. Reread Exercise 3 on page 172. Then ask your partner about his or her grandparents or other older relatives. With the class, talk about life in the past. In what ways was it different from today?

REVIEW OR SELFTEST

PART V

I. *Read each conversation. Circle the letter of the the underlined word or group of words that is not correct.*

1. **A:** You <u>didn't</u> <u>finished</u> your dinner.
             A   B

   B: That's because <u>it</u> <u>wasn't</u> good.
                  C   D

   A B C D

2. **A:** <u>Who(m)</u> <u>you</u> <u>did</u> call?
          A   B

   B: I <u>called</u> John. I <u>wanted</u> Susan's phone number.
         C   D

   A B C D

3. **A:** When <u>did</u> they <u>visit</u> Hawaii?
           A   B

   B: They <u>visit</u> Hawaii last fall. They <u>were</u> there for
          C   D

   a week.

   A B C D

4. **A:** <u>How long</u> did <u>it took</u> you to get to work?
       A   B

   B: <u>It took</u> me over an hour. <u>Traffic was</u> very heavy.
        C   B

   A B C D

5. **A:** <u>Did</u> she <u>drank</u> a glass of milk?
       A   B

   B: Yes. She <u>drank</u> it with some cookies. Then she <u>did</u>
             C   D

   her homework.

   A B C D

6. **A:** Where <u>did</u> you <u>see</u> them?
          A   B

   B: I <u>did</u> <u>saw</u> them during the Thanksgiving vacation.
      C   D

   A B C D

II. *Read each question. Circle the correct answer.*

1. When did you get up?
   a. At eight-thirty.
   b. Yes, I did.
   c. Because it was early.

2. Who visited us last week?
   a. They do.
   b. They were.
   c. They did.

3. Where did they go yesterday?
   a. To the movies.
   b. At noon.
   c. With their friends.

4. Did they have a good breakfast?
   a. Yes, they do.
   b. Yes, they had.
   c. Yes, they did.

5. How long did she stay?
   a. By bus.
   b. A few hours.
   c. An hour ago.

6. Did she have a good vacation last summer?
   a. No, she hasn't.
   b. No, she didn't.
   c. No, she wasn't.

7. Who did you stay with?
   a. My relatives.
   b. John did.
   c. On Saturday.

8. Did it rain last night?
   a. No, it doesn't.
   b. No, it didn't.
   c. No, it don't.

III. *Complete the story. Use the past tense of each verb in parentheses.*

George Washington was the first president of the United States.

He _____ in a beautiful home in Virginia. His
   1. (live)
mother _____ a special garden with a beautiful little
   2. (have)
cherry tree. Everyone _____ that cherry tree. One day
   3. (love)
George _____ a hatchet as a present. He _____
   4. (get)   5. (decide)
to try the hatchet. He _____ to the cherry tree and
   6. (go)
_____ it down. As soon as he _____ the tree on the ground,
   7. (chop)   8. (see)
he _____ terrible. He _____ sadly back to the house
   9. (feel)   10. (walk)
and _____ to his room. He _____ that afternoon. He
   11. (go)   12. (play, not)
_____ that evening. That night George's father said, "Someone
   13. (eat not)
_____ down our cherry tree." George _____ to tell his father
   14. (chop)   15. (decide)
the truth. He _____ toward his father and said, "I _____ it.
   16. (walk)   17. (chop)
I _____ it down with my new hatchet. I cannot tell a lie."
   18. (chop)
   "Thank you for telling the truth," his father _____.
                                                   19. (say)

IV. *Complete the conversations. Use the simple present, present progressive, or simple past form of each verb in parentheses.*

1. A: Why (arrive) _____ you _____ so late?

   B: I (forget) _____ to set my alarm clock last night.

2. A: There aren't any grapes. Who (eat) _____ them all?

   B: I don't know. I (eat, not) _____ them. I (like, not) _____ grapes.

(continued on next page)

3. A: I (get) _____ a beautiful gift in the mail last week.

   B: Who (send) _____ it?

   A: Uncle Sam.

4. A: What (say) _____ his answering machine _____?

   B: It says, "I'm sorry I (miss) _____ your call. Please leave your name and a

   short message. Thank you. Have a nice day."

5. A: Let's study together.

   B: Gee, I'm not in the mood to study. I (study) _____ all day yesterday.

   What (do) _____ you _____ yesterday?

   A: I (play) _____ tennis.

6. A: Where are the kids?

   B: Annie (play) _____ outside, and Dave (do) _____ homework.

   A: What about Annie's homework?

   B: She (do) _____ it last night.

7. A: Where are the cookies?

   B: I (hide) _____ them last night.

   A: Why (hide) _____ you _____ them?

   B: I (try) _____ to lose weight.

   A: Well, I'm not. I (want) _____ those cookies.

V. *Complete each sentence. Choose the correct time marker. Write it on the line.*

1. _____ I wash my clothes.
   a. A week ago   **b.** Every Monday

2. Did you see your friend _____?
   a. this morning   **b.** now

3. We visited them two weeks _____.
   a. last   **b.** ago

4. I spoke to the doctor _____ Thursday.
   a. last   **b.** ago

▶ *To check your answers, go to the Answer Key on page 181.*

FROM GRAMMAR TO WRITING
PUNCTUATION II:
The Exclamation Point (!), The Hyphen (-), Quotation Marks (" . . . ")

1 *What's wrong with these sentences?*

1. You're kidding

2. She's twenty one years old

3. He said I love you

4. He worked for many years before he became rich.

Study this information about punctuation. Then add the correct
punctuation to the sentences above.

The Exclamation Point (!)

1. Use the exclamation point
after **strong**, **emotional
statements**. (Don't use it
too often.)

- What a surprise!
- You're kidding!
- How wonderful!

The Hyphen (-)

2. a. Use a hyphen in
compound numbers
from twenty-one to
ninety-nine.

- There were **twenty-two**
students in the class.

b. Use a hyphen **at the end
of a line** when dividing
a word. Words must be
divided by syllables.
(Check your dictionary.
If you are unsure, do not
hyphenate words.)

- We visited them at the **beginning** of the year.

(continued on next page)

179

Quotation Marks (" . . . ")

3. Use quotation marks **before** and **after the exact words** of a speaker. Use a comma before the quote.

- She said, "I just love your new sweater."

---

2 *Last week the students in Al Brown's English class told stories they heard as children. Maria told the class a story from the Bible. Read the story. Circle the exclamation marks and hyphens. Add quotation marks where necessary.*

WHOSE BABY IS IT?

Solomon was a king. He lived about 3,000 years ago. Everyone came to Solomon because he was very wise.

One day two women approached King Solomon. One carried a baby. The first woman said, We live nearby and had our babies three days apart. Her baby died in the night, and she changed it for mine. This baby is really mine.

King Solomon turned to the other woman. She said, No! That woman is lying. That's my baby.

The two women started shouting and continued until King Solomon shout-ed, Stop!

He then turned to his guard and said, Take your sword and chop the baby in two. Give one part to this woman and the other to that one. The guard pul-led out his sword. As he was about to divide the baby, the first woman screamed, No! Don't do it. Give her the baby. Just don't kill the baby.

King Solomon then said, Now I know the mother. Give the baby to the woman who has just spoken.

---

3 *Work in small groups.*

1. *Brainstorm.*

What was your favorite story as a child?

When did you first hear it? Who told it to you? Why did you like it?

2. *Tell your story to your group.*

3. *Write your story. When you are finished, read your story twice. First read it for the story. Next read it for grammar and punctuation.*

4. *Rewrite your story. Hang it on the wall. Go around and read the stories of your classmates.*

I.
1. B
2. B
3. C
4. B
5. B
6. C

II.
1. a
2. c
3. a
4. c
5. b
6. b
7. a
8. b

III.
1. lived
2. had
3. loved
4. got
5. decided
6. went
7. chopped
8. saw
9. felt
10. walked
11. went
12. didn't play
13. didn't eat
14. chopped
15. decided
16. walked
17. chopped
18. chopped
19. said

IV.
1. did arrive, forgot
2. ate, didn't eat, don't like
3. got, sent
4. does, say, missed
5. studied, did, do, played
6. 's playing (is playing), 's doing (is doing), did
7. hid, did, hide, 'm trying (am trying), want

V.
1. b
2. a
3. b
4. a

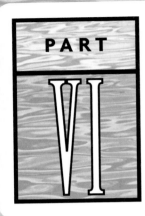

IMPERATIVES; SUGGESTIONS; THERE IS / THERE ARE

PREVIEW

Elenore and Pete are walking along Third Avenue in New York City. Listen and read their conversation.

LET'S STOP FOR PIZZA

ELENORE: What a beautiful day!

PETE: It sure is. There isn't a cloud in the sky!

ELENORE: I'm getting hungry. Let's stop for pizza.

PETE: Okay. But are there any pizza places around here?

ELENORE: I don't know. There's a young man there. Why don't you ask him?

PETE: Excuse me. Is there a pizza place near here?

YOUNG MAN: Sorry, I don't think so. There's a Chinese restaurant on this street, and there are several small restaurants on the next street. There are a few coffee bars on 43rd Street, but I don't know of any pizza places near here.

PETE: Thanks anyway. Elenore, there's a woman over there. Ask her.

ELENORE: Excuse me. Are there any pizza places near here?

WOMAN: Not here, but Luigi's is on 37th Street and Third. Just walk down Third Avenue. Then turn right on 37th Street. Luigi's has great pizza.

ELENORE: Thanks a lot.

[20 minutes later]

PETE: There it is.

ELENORE: Finally! I'm hungry and tired.

PETE: Uh-oh.

ELENORE: What's wrong?

PETE: Look! "Closed for Renovations."

COMPREHENSION CHECK

Complete the sentences. Circle the right words.

1. Elenore and Pete walk to Luigi's Pizza because _____.
   a. it's the only restaurant in the area
   b. Luigi is their friend
   c. a woman tells them that Luigi's has great pizza

2. Elenore and Pete didn't have pizza because _____.
   a. they were tired and wanted to go home
   b. the pizza place wasn't open
   c. there weren't any pizza places there

WITH PARTNERS

Practice the conversation on pages 182 and 183.

IMPERATIVES; SUGGESTIONS WITH LET'S, WHY DON'T WE . . . ?; WHY DON'T YOU . . . ?

GRAMMAR **IN CONTEXT**

WARM UP   People eat pizza all over the world. Some say it's the first global food. What do you think about pizza? Do you like it? What's your favorite kind?

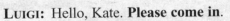
Listen and read about today's person in the news.

The Daily Times   Section 2/Page 3

PERSON IN THE NEWS

Today's "Person in the News" is Luigi Paolini. Ten years ago, Luigi came to New York from Naples and opened a tiny pizza shop. Today Luigi has five pizzerias in New York City. Our reporter, Kate Evans, interviewed Luigi in his 37th Street store.

LUIGI: Hello, Kate. **Please come in**.

KATE: Wow. It's busy here.

LUIGI: Yes. We're expanding.
Sorry, Kate. It's noisy and messy. **Please be** careful. **Don't touch** anything. . . . **Why don't we step** into my office?

KATE: Good idea. **Let's go**. . . . Luigi, your pizza is a big success. How come?

LUIGI: Well, my food is fresh and my prices are low. But I think the real reason is the dough.

KATE: The dough?

LUIGI: Uh-huh. My grandpa taught me the secret.

KATE: Would you share the recipe?

LUIGI: Sure. But that's not the secret. The secret is how I handle the dough.

LUIGI'S PIZZA DOUGH	
Ingredients:	Directions:
1 package of fast-acting yeast	1. **Stir** the yeast and sugar into the water. **Wait** five minutes.
1 teaspoon sugar	2. **Put** the flour, oil, and salt in a food processor.
1 cup warm water	**Add** the ingredients in #1. **Turn on** the food
1 cup flour	processor for 40 seconds. Now you have the dough.
2 tablespoons olive oil	3. **Put** the dough in a large plastic food bag. **Place** the bag in a bowl. **Leave** it in the bowl for one hour. (It will rise.)
1 teaspoon salt	4. **Make** two large pizza crusts or three small ones.

Match the pictures and the directions.

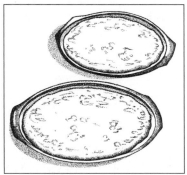

a. _____

c. _____

b. _____

d. _____

GRAMMAR **PRESENTATION**
IMPERATIVES; SUGGESTIONS WITH *LET'S, WHY DON'T WE . . . ?*;
ADVICE WITH *WHY DON'T YOU . . . ?*

IMPERATIVES

AFFIRMATIVE	
BASE FORM OF VERB	
Open	the door.

NEGATIVE		
DON'T	**BASE FORM OF VERB**	
Don't	**open**	the door.

SUGGESTIONS

AFFIRMATIVE		
LET'S	**BASE FORM OF VERB**	
Let's	**take**	a walk.

NEGATIVE			
LET'S	*NOT*	**BASE FORM OF VERB**	
Let's	**not**	**take**	a walk.

WHY DON'T WE	**BASE FORM OF VERB**	**. . . ?**
Why don't we	**order**	pizza?

ADVICE

WHY DON'T YOU	**BASE FORM OF VERB**	**. . . ?**
Why don't you	**take**	a break?

NOTES	EXAMPLES
1. The **imperative** uses the **base form of the verb**. The base form is the form in the dictionary. For example: *Walk* is the base form of the verb *walk*. (Other forms are *walking*, *walks*, and *walked*.)	• **Walk** three blocks and **turn** right.
2. Use the imperative to: **a.** give **directions** and **instructions**. **b.** give **orders** or **commands**. **c.** give **advice** or make **suggestions**. **d.** give **warnings**. **e.** make **polite requests**.	• **Stir** the sugar in the water. • **Be** quiet! • **Relax**. • **Keep** out! Danger! • **Please open** the door.
3. *Don't* comes before the base form for the negative imperative.	• **Don't turn** left.
4. In an imperative statement, the subject is always *you*, but we don't say it or write it.	• **Ask** that young man. (You) ask that young man.
5. Use *Let's* or *Let's not* and the base form for suggestions that include you and another person.	• **Let's go**. • **Let's not stay**.
6. Use *Why don't we* and the base form for suggestions that include you and another person. Use *Why don't you* and the base form to give advice to another person. REMEMBER: to put a question mark at the end of sentences with *Why don't we* and *Why don't you*.	• **Why don't we go** to my office? • **Why don't you look** on the Internet?

FOCUSED PRACTICE

1 DISCOVER THE GRAMMAR

While Elenore and Pete were walking along Third Avenue, two burglars entered their home. Listen and read their conversation. Then underline the imperatives.

FRANK: Hey, George. I'm nervous. This is my first job.

GEORGE: <u>Relax</u>, Frank. I'm here.

FRANK: Okay, George. What's this? Is this a gold watch?

GEORGE: Yes, it's gold. Take it.

FRANK: How about these pearls next to the watch?

GEORGE: They're good pearls. Put them in our bag.

FRANK: What's that, over there?

GEORGE: Junk. Don't take it.

FRANK: What's under the junk?

GEORGE: It's a ring, but leave it. It's a cheap ring.

FRANK: Are these good earrings?

GEORGE: Yes, give them to me.

FRANK: What's that noise?

GEORGE: A police siren. Drop everything. Let's run!

How many imperatives are there?

a. 5   **b.** 7   **c.** 8

2 TELEPHONE MESSAGES

Elenore and Pete are now home. Listen to their conversation.

Now listen to their conversation again, complete the chart, and answer the question.

	WHO CALLED?	**WHAT'S THE MESSAGE?**	**WHAT'S THE CALLER'S NUMBER?**
Message 1			
Message 2			
Message 3			

Why didn't the third caller leave a telephone number?

3 GIVING DIRECTIONS

Grammar Notes 1–2, 4

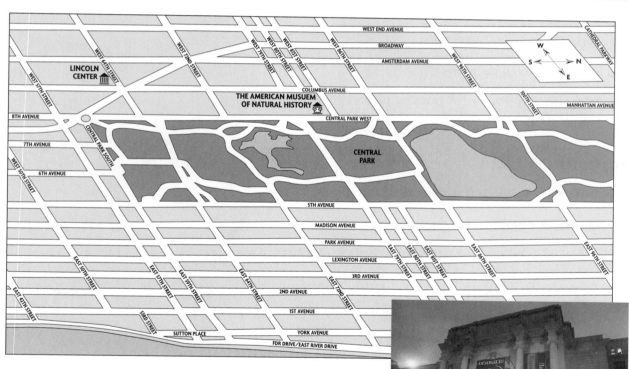

A visitor to New York asks Doug for directions to the American Museum of Natural History. Read their conversation and look at the map. Where is this conversation taking place?

Doug and the visitor are at _____ .

VISITOR: Excuse me, how can I get to the American Museum of Natural History?

DOUG: Do you want to walk or take the subway?

VISITOR: Is it in walking distance?

(continued on next page)

DOUG: Yes—it's just about a mile.

VISITOR: Then I'll walk.

DOUG: Okay. Go down to 81st Street.

VISITOR: Is that south?

DOUG: Yes, walk fifteen blocks. Turn left on 81st Street. Walk three blocks until you get to Central Park West. Turn right and you're at the main entrance to the museum.

VISITOR: Thanks.

Now look at the map and write directions to Lincoln Center from the American Museum of Natural History. The entrance to Lincoln Center is on Columbus Avenue and 64th Street. You are leaving the museum at 80th Street and Central Park West.

4 EDITING

A young man delivers a pizza. Find and correct the six mistakes.

WOMAN: Who's there?

YOUNG MAN: Pizza delivery.

WOMAN: Oh. Please to put the pizza down here. How much do I owe you?

YOUNG MAN: $16.95.

WOMAN: Here's $20. Keeps the change.

YOUNG MAN: Thanks. Excuse me, what's the best way to get to 115 East 79th Street?

WOMAN: Driving up First Avenue to 79th Street and turning left.

YOUNG MAN: Thanks.

WOMAN: Is your car in a parking spot?

YOUNG MAN: Yes.

WOMAN: Then why you don't walk? It's only three blocks from here. Parking is very difficult.

YOUNG MAN: Good idea. It's a beautiful night.

WOMAN: No mention it.

COMMUNICATION PRACTICE

5 FINDING IMPERATIVES

Work in small groups. Look at the instructions in this textbook and find imperative statements. Write down ten base-form verbs used in the instructions. Read your list to the other groups.

1. _____work_____   6. _____

2. _____   7. _____

3. _____   8. _____

4. _____   9. _____

5. _____   10. _____

6 MAKING SUGGESTIONS / GIVING ADVICE

Work with a partner.

A. *Make three suggestions for each situation. Begin with* **Let's** *or* **Why don't we**. *Use the ideas in the box or your own ideas.*

> go to the movies, the theater, a concert, the park
> play ball, tennis, soccer
> have a party

A: The weather is great.   **A:** There's no school tomorrow.

B: _____   **B:** _____

B. *Advise someone with the following problems. Begin with* **Why don't you**. *Use the ideas in the box or your own ideas.*

> take a course in Swedish   ask friends about their computers
> visit Sweden   read about computers
> get some Swedish tapes   go to stores and ask questions about computers

A: I want to learn Swedish.   **A:** I want to buy a computer.

B: _____   **B:** _____

Your idea:

A: _I want_____

B: _____

7 GAME: SIMON SAYS

Work with a partner. Label the parts of the body. (See Appendix 5 on page A-5 to check your work.)

head	hip
shoulder	knee
ankle	stomach
back	thigh
waist	toe

*Play a game. A leader (a student or the teacher) goes to the front of the class. The leader makes polite requests (using **please**) and commands.*

EXAMPLE:

Please put your hands on your knees. *(polite request)*

Put your hands on your ankles. *(command)*

*The class follows only the polite requests (when the leader says **please**). If a student follows a command, the student sits down. The last student standing becomes the next leader.*

8 WITH A PARTNER

Work in pairs. Give directions to your partner to . . .

1. your home from school
2. a good restaurant from school

EXAMPLE:

A: How can I get to your home from school?

B: Take the number 4 train and get off at 14th Street. Walk one block south to 13th Street. Then turn right. I live at 124 East 13th Street.

SUBJECT AND OBJECT PRONOUNS; DIRECT AND INDIRECT OBJECTS

GRAMMAR **IN CONTEXT**

WARM UP   Do you know a few sentences in different languages? What languages? Who taught them to you?

Listen and read the conversation between Carol and Yoko.

CAROL: This is a great picture of you. Who are **you** standing with?

YOKO: Bekir and Maria. Do **you** know **them**?

CAROL: I know **him**. **He**'s the guy from Turkey. But **I** don't think **I** know **her**. Who is Maria?

YOKO: **She**'s a friend from Brazil. I met **her** in the library. **She** wants to learn **Japanese**. I'm teaching **her some Japanese**. And **she**'s teaching **me a little Portuguese**.

CAROL: That's great. Where was this picture taken?

YOKO: In Bekir's apartment.

CAROL: What's **he** wearing?

YOKO: **It**'s my yutaka. My mom sent **it to me** last month.

CAROL: **He** looks cute in **it**.

Tudo bem

Tudo bem

YOKO: I know. I told **him**. I **lent it to him** for the International Students Masquerade Party last Saturday, and he won **first prize**.

CAROL: No kidding! That's cool.

Hajimemashite

Hajimemashite

GRAMMAR **PRESENTATION**
SUBJECT AND OBJECT PRONOUNS; DIRECT AND INDIRECT OBJECTS

SUBJECT AND OBJECT PRONOUNS

SINGULAR			
SUBJECT PRONOUN AND VERB			**OBJECT PRONOUN**
I'm **You**'re **He**'s **She**'s	happy.	He likes	**me**. **you**. **him**. **her**. **it**.
It's	wonderful.		

PLURAL			
SUBJECT PRONOUN AND VERB			**OBJECT PRONOUN**
We're **You**'re **They**'re	happy.	He likes	**us**. **you**. **them**.

DIRECT AND INDIRECT OBJECTS

SUBJECT	VERB	DIRECT OBJECT	*To*	INDIRECT OBJECT	SUBJECT	VERB	INDIRECT OBJECT	DIRECT OBJECT
She	**sent**	**a gift** **it**	**to**	**us**.	She	**sent**	**us**	**a gift**.

NOTES	EXAMPLES
1. A pronoun replaces a noun. A **subject pronoun** replaces a noun in subject position.	subject • **Carol** loves Rocky. • **She** loves Rocky.

2. An **object pronoun** replaces a noun in object position (after the verb).

object
- Carol loves **Rocky**.
- She loves **him**.

3. When you refer to yourself and another person, the other person comes first.

- **Carol and I** love Rocky.
  NOT ~~I and Carol love Rocky.~~

4. Some sentences have only a subject and a verb.

Some sentences have a subject, a verb, and an object.

Some sentences have two objects following the verb.

A **direct object** answers the question *whom* or *what*.

An **indirect object** answers the question *to whom* or *to what*.

subject   verb
- Pete painted.

subject   verb   object
- Yoko's mom sent **a yutaka**.

subject   verb   object   indirect object
- Yoko's mom sent **a yutaka to Yoko**.

- **What** did Yoko's mom send?
                                    direct object
  Yoko's mom sent **a yutaka**.

- **To whom** did she send the yutaka?
                                         indirect object
- Yoko's mom sent the yutaka **to Yoko**.

5. For the verbs *give, hand, lend, pass, read, sell, send, show, write, teach, tell, throw, owe,* and *e-mail,* there are two possible sentence patterns if the direct object is a noun.

direct object   indirect
(noun)   *to*   object
- She gave **the yutaka to her**.

OR

indirect   direct object
object   (noun)
- She gave **her the yutaka**.

If the direct object is a **pronoun**, it always comes before the indirect object.

direct object   indirect
(pronoun)   *to*   object
- She gave   **it**   **to her**.

FOCUSED PRACTICE

① DISCOVER THE GRAMMAR

*Read each sentence. Write **d** above the direct object and **i** above the indirect object. Circle the subject pronouns. Underline the object pronouns.*

1. Show the book to me.

2. They told us the truth.

3. Write me a letter.

4. Show your work to your partner.

5. We threw the ball to them.

6. She read us the message.

② UNDERSTANDING DIRECTIONS   Grammar Note 2

*Complete the sentences. Use **me**, **him**, **her**, **it**, **you**, **us**, or **them**. Then draw a line from the object pronoun to the noun or pronoun it replaces.*

1. Find the pronouns. Then circle _____them_____.

2. Underline the sentence. Then circle _____.

3. Read this story. Read _____ to the class.

4. Al Brown is helpful. Ask _____ for help.

5. Please don't help _____. We want to work alone.

6. I'm lost. Please help _____.

7. Carol is good at drawing. Ask _____ to draw it for you.

8. Carol and I are good at drawing. Ask _____ to draw those cartoons for you.

9. Yoko and Ali are good at grammar. Ask _____ for help.

10. There are two bananas on the counter. Please don't eat _____.

3 HELPING OTHERS

Complete the conversations. Use subject and object pronouns.

1. **CAROL:** Yoko, _____I_____'m wet. Please give

   _____me_____ a towel.

   YOKO: Here __you__ are.

2. **LULU:** This little boy is on the wrong bus.

   _____'s lost. Please help _____.

   BUS DRIVER: Okay, son. Where are _____ going?

3. **MILT:** Excuse me. We're looking for an

   express train. Can you help _____?

   WOMAN: The express train stops there. Look!

   There _____ is.

4. **ELENORE:** Paul and Mary bought the same

   computer that we did. They're

   having trouble with _____. Please

   show _____ how it works.

   PETE: No problem.

4 IN OTHER WORDS

Underline the direct object in each sentence. Then complete the conversations.
*Use **it** or **them** in place of the direct object. (Remember: When the direct object is*
a pronoun, it always comes before the indirect object.)

1. A: I gave my brother my bicycle.

   B: Who did you give it to?

   A: _I gave it to my brother._____

2. A: I handed my boss my report.

   B: Who did you hand it to?

   A: _____

(continued on next page)

3. A: She owes her roommate a lot of money.

   B: Who does she owe a lot of money to?

   A: _____

4. A: Please pass Yoko the salt.

   B: What do you want me to do with the salt?

   A: _____

5 EDITING

Read this conversation between Carol and Dan. Find and correct the four errors.

CAROL: Ron's parents are very generous.

   DAN: Oh? Why do you say that?

CAROL: Well, last month they gave him a car. The year before they sent to Europe him.

   And they often give he expensive gifts.

   DAN: They *are* generous. Ron's lucky. Is he grateful?

CAROL: No. He thinks they owe it to him.

   DAN: I'd like to introduce him to Jack's parents.

CAROL: Why?

   DAN: Well, last summer Jack gave their parents a new car. And he sent them to Hawaii

   on their anniversary.

CAROL: What a nice guy.

   DAN: I know, but his parents think he owes them it.

COMMUNICATION PRACTICE

6 DOING SOMETHING NICE FOR A CLASSMATE

Work in small groups. Discuss things you can do for classmates. Use the
verbs **give**, **lend**, **send**, **write**, *and* **e-mail** *in your conversations.*

A classmate is sick.

A classmate's birthday is soon.

A classmate needs a suit for a job interview.

> **EXAMPLE:**
> Let's send him some cards.
> Why don't we give him a gift?

7 GAME

Throw a ball (or pass a message or tell a secret) to a student. That student throws
the ball to another student. Continue four more times. The last person tells the
class who threw the ball (or passed the message or told the secret) to whom.

> **EXAMPLE:**
> José threw it to Erica. Erica threw it to Ali. Ali . . .

8 GIFTS, CARDS, E-MAIL, AND LETTERS

Work in small groups. Talk about the people to whom you give gifts, cards, e-mail messages, and letters.

1. I usually give presents to _____.

2. I send greeting cards to _____.

3. I write letters to _____.

4. I e-mail messages to _____.

Then tell your group about a special card or present that you gave someone or someone gave you.

EXAMPLE:

When my son was four years old, he had a friend from Pakistan. Every day when I took my son to the park, his friend asked to go along. His mother rarely left her home. I never knew why. At the end of the summer, the family moved. When we said good-bye, the mother gave me a very beautiful hand-carved lamp. Whenever I see the lamp, I remember the boy and his mother.

THERE IS / THERE ARE, IS THERE . . . ? / ARE THERE . . . ?

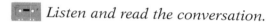

GRAMMAR **IN CONTEXT**

WARM UP   There are shopping malls all over the world. They attract people of all ages and incomes. Do you shop at malls? Why or why not? Are there any near your home?

Listen and read the conversation.

MAN: Excuse me. **Is there** a mall around here?

WOMAN: Yes. **There's** a huge mall just up ahead. Follow me. I'm going **there**.

MAN: **Is there** a restaurant at the mall?

WOMAN: **There are** at least five different fast food places at the food court.

MAN: **Are there** any nice restaurants?

WOMAN: I'm not sure. I think **there's** one nice restaurant. Anyway, when you get to the mall, go to the third floor. All the food is **there**.

MAN: Thanks.

GRAMMAR **PRESENTATION**
THERE IS / THERE ARE, IS THERE . . . ? / ARE THERE . . . ?

THERE IS / THERE ARE

AFFIRMATIVE			
THERE	**BE**	**SUBJECT**	**PLACE**
There	**is**	a restaurant	on this street.
There	**are**	two restaurants	

CONTRACTIONS	
there is	→ **there's**
there is not	→ **there isn't**
there are not	→ **there aren't**

NEGATIVE			
THERE	**BE**	**SUBJECT**	**PLACE**
There	**isn't**	a good restaurant	on this street.
There	**aren't**	any good restaurants	

IS THERE . . . ? / ARE THERE . . . ?

QUESTIONS			
BE	**THERE**	**SUBJECT**	**PLACE**
Is	**there**	a pizza place	near here?
Are	**there**	any banks	

SHORT ANSWERS	
AFFIRMATIVE	**NEGATIVE**
Yes, there is.	No, there isn't.
Yes, there are.	No, there aren't.

NOTES	EXAMPLES
1. Use *there is* or *there's* to say that a person or thing is somewhere.	• **There's** a man at the door.
2. Use *there are* to say that people or things are somewhere.	• **There are** five fast food places in the mall.
▶ **BE CAREFUL!** Don't confuse *there are* and *they are*.	subject • **There are** ten women in our class. subject • **They are** all good students.
3. In the negative, use the contractions *isn't* and *aren't*. The full forms, *is not* and *are not*, are rarely used with *there*.	• **There isn't** a cloud in the sky. • **There aren't** any malls near our school.
4. We usually use *any* with *yes / no* questions about plural nouns.	• Are there **any** malls nearby?
5. BE CAREFUL! Don't confuse *there is* and *there are* with *there*. (The last *there* in the example sentence points out something that is not nearby. We use *here* for something nearby.)	• Oregon is a beautiful place. **There are** mountains and beaches *there*. • Last summer we exchanged homes with friends in Lisbon. We went **there** and they came **here**.

FOCUSED PRACTICE

DISCOVER THE GRAMMAR

Look at the mall directory. Check the sentences that are true.

Mall Directory

Third Floor	3a	3b	3c	3d	3e	
Food Court	Thai food	Chinese food	Burgers	Sushi bar	Coffee bar	
Second Floor	2a	2b	2c	2d	2e	2f
	Women's clothes	Shoe store	Art supply store	Furniture store	Children's clothes	Cosmetics store
First Floor	1a	1b	1c	1d	1e	1f
	Florist	Gift shop	Bookstore	Unisex hair salon	Electronics store	Women's clothes

_____ 1. There's a florist on the first floor.

_____ 2. There's a coffee bar on the second floor.

_____ 3. There aren't any toy stores.

_____ 4. There are five places to eat.

_____ 5. There isn't any Thai food at this mall.

_____ 6. There's a bookstore on the first floor.

2 WORD ORDER PRACTICE
Grammar Notes 1–4

Put a check (✔) next to each correct sentence. Change sentences that don't make sense.

_____ 1. There's a mall in the Chinese restaurant. _There's a Chinese Restaurant in the mall._

_____ 2. There's a second floor on the gift shop. _____

_____ 3. There are two women's clothes stores at the mall. _____

_____ 4. There's an electronics store on the first floor. _____

_____ 5. There isn't any mall at the men's clothing store. _____

3 A TERRIBLE PIZZA PLACE

Complete the sentences. Use **there isn't**, **there aren't**, *or* **they aren't**.

ALLEN: This pizza place is terrible. _____ any tablecloths and the placemats

         1.

         are dirty.

NORMA: You're right. _____ any napkins, either.

         2.

ALLEN: There are real knives and forks, but _____ clean.

         3.

NORMA: There are waiters, but _____ very polite.

         4.

ALLEN: It's very hot, but _____ even a fan.

         5.

NORMA: Let's leave.

4 HOW ABOUT SOME MEXICAN FOOD?

Complete the conversation. Use **there's**, **there are**, **they're**, *and* **there**.

DAHLIA: Are you in the mood for pizza?

NORMA: Let's not have pizza. I was at a terrible pizza place yesterday. _____

                                                               1.

         lots of other restaurants around.

DAHLIA: Today is Sunday. Are any of them open?

NORMA: _____ all open seven days a week.

         2.

DAHLIA: How about a Mexican restaurant? _____ a good one on the next street.

                                                             3.

NORMA: Great. I love Mexican food and I know that restaurant. I was _____

                                                                      4.

         a few months ago.

5 EDITING

Find and correct the three mistakes in this reading.

Pizzas come in all shapes and sizes. Are pizzas with mushrooms, with pepperoni, with
broccoli, and with tofu. In the United States they are over 61,000 pizzerias. Their sales
reach 30 billion dollars. People in the United States eat 3 billion pizzas a year. They are
pizza shops in almost every city, town, and village.

COMMUNICATION PRACTICE

6 GAME: ARE THERE ANY TWINS IN YOUR FAMILY?

Use the phrases in the boxes and ask your classmates questions. Begin with **Is there** *or* **Are there any**. *If a student says* yes, *write his or her name in the box. When you have three across or down, call out "I've got it!"*

twins in your family	famous people in your family	detectives in your family
a plant in your home	a black comb in your pocket	pictures in your wallet
a Thai restaurant near your home	pizza places on your street	park near your home

EXAMPLE:

A: Are there any twins in your family?

B: Yes. My mother is a twin. *(A writes B's name in the first box.)*

7 INFORMATION GAP: IS THERE A CLOCK IN THE KITCHEN?

Work in pairs.

Student A, your partner has a picture of a kitchen and a dining room. Ask your partner if the following items are in the kitchen or the dining room. Write the name of the room (or rooms) they are in. Cross out items that are not in your partner's picture.

Student B, turn to the Information Gap on pages 222 and 223 and follow the instructions there.

EXAMPLE:

A: Is there a dining room table in the dining room?

B: Yes, there is.

1. dining room table <u>dining room</u>

2. chairs _____

3. calendar _____

4. refrigerator _____

5. pictures _____

6. stove _____

7. dishwasher _____

8. microwave oven _____

9. toaster _____

10. clock _____

11. cabinets _____

12. counter _____

13. chandelier _____

14. rug _____

Student A, you have a picture of a living room and a bedroom. Answer your partner's questions about your picture.

8 **A ROOM IN MY HOME**

Work with a partner. Take turns. Describe a room in your home. Your partner draws it. Check each other's drawings.

24 NUMBERS, QUANTIFIERS, AND QUESTIONS WITH *HOW MANY . . . ?*

GRAMMAR **IN CONTEXT**

WARM UP   Is there a cafeteria in your school? Do you have any complaints about it? If yes, what are they?

Carol and Connie are in line at their school cafeteria. Listen and read their conversation.

CONNIE: Hi Carol.

CAROL: Oh, hi Connie. How's it going?

CONNIE: Okay. What are you having for lunch?

CAROL: A hamburger and fries.

CONNIE: Hmm. **There aren't many** choices.

CAROL: What do you mean? **There are five** choices. There are hamburgers, chicken, pasta, fish, and pizza. **How many** do you want?

CONNIE: Well, I want fish, but **there's** only **one** kind of fish.

CAROL: Oh.

CONNIE: And **there aren't any** limes.

CAROL: Limes?

CONNIE: For the fish.

CAROL: But **there are lots of** lemons.

CONNIE: I like limes. What's for dessert?

CAROL: **There are a lot of** desserts. **There are four** different pies, **some** apples, **a few** cupcakes, and **several** kinds of cookies. What are you looking for?

CONNIE: Cherry pie. **There isn't any** cherry pie.

CAROL: Then I guess there's no dessert for you.

CONNIE: I'll settle for a cookie. And maybe a small slice of apple pie.

WHAT'S YOUR OPINION?

Are Connie's complaints reasonable?

GRAMMAR **PRESENTATION**
NUMBERS, QUANTIFIERS, AND QUESTIONS WITH *HOW MANY . . . ?*

NUMBERS AND QUANTIFIERS

AFFIRMATIVE		
SINGULAR		
There's	**a** **one**	mistake.

NEGATIVE		
SINGULAR		
There	**isn't a** **isn't one**	mistake.
There's	**no**	

AFFIRMATIVE		
PLURAL		
There are	**four** **a few** **some** **several** **many** **a lot of** **lots of**	mistakes.

NEGATIVE		
PLURAL		
There	are **no** aren**'t any** aren**'t many** aren**'t a lot of**	mistakes.

HOW MANY . . . ?

QUESTIONS			
HOW MANY	**PLURAL NOUN**	*BE THERE*	
How many	restaurants	**are there**	in this area?

ANSWERS
There are eight restaurants in this area.
There are eight.
Eight.
There are a lot.
There's one.
There aren't any.

NOTES	EXAMPLES
1. Use **articles, numbers**, or **quantifiers** with *there's, there are, there isn't,* and *there aren't.*	• **There's a** fly in your soup. *(article)* • **There are three** worms in these apples. *(number)* • **There aren't many** people in this restaurant. *(quantifier)*
2. For the **negative**, we usually say *There aren't any*. *There isn't a, There are no, There's no*, or *There isn't one* are usually used for emphasis.	• **There aren't any** limes. • **There isn't a** thing to eat. • **There are no** carrots. • **There's no** milk! • **There isn't one** piece of bread.
3. Use *a lot of* and *many* for large numbers. Use *lots of* in speaking and very informal writing.	• **There are a lot of** carrots in this soup. • **There are lots of** carrots in this soup.
4. Use *a few* and *not many* for small numbers.	• **There are a few** oranges. • **There aren't many** apples.
5. Use numbers or quantifiers in answers to questions with *how many*.	**A:** How many people are there? **B:** Four. OR **A few.**

REFERENCE NOTE
See Unit 33 and 34 for more notes about quantifiers.
See Unit 34 for questions with *how much*.

FOCUSED PRACTICE

① DISCOVER THE GRAMMAR

Look at the picture.

Choose the answer that completes the sentences.

1. There's one _____ .

2. There are several _____ .

3. There aren't any _____ .

4. There are a lot of _____ .

a. parking meters

b. people

c. toy stores

d. bakery

② A BUSY STREET
Grammar Note 5

Write questions about the underlined words. Begin with **How many** *and other*
wh- *questions.*

1. There's <u>one pizza place</u>. _____

2. <u>A hardware store</u> is next to the supermarket. _____

_____

3. There are <u>six parking meters</u> on the street. _____

4. The pizza place is <u>between the shoe repair store and the hardware store</u>. _____

_____

3 **A FRUIT BOWL**

*Look at the picture and complete the sentences. Use **There aren't any**, **There are a few**, **There are a lot of**, or **There is one**, **There are two***.

1. ___There are a few___ apples.

2. _____ pears.

3. _____ grapes.

4. _____ banana.

5. _____ pineapples.

6. _____ watermelons.

7. _____ oranges.

4 **TEST RESULTS**

Al Brown is returning tests. Listen and match the names with the grades.

_____ **1.** Yoko   **a.** 100 percent

_____ **2.** Bekir   **b.** 99 percent

_____ **3.** Yolanda   **c.** 66 percent

_____ **4.** Michiko   **d.** 85 percent

COMMUNICATION PRACTICE

5 GUESS THE NUMBER

Guess how many of each item there are in your classroom. Work quickly. Don't count. Then count the items with the class and compare the correct number to your guesses.

EXAMPLE:
How many desks are there?
Your guess: 20
Class count: 23

	Your guess	Class count			Your guess	Class count
1. chairs	_____	_____	**6.** umbrellas		_____	_____
2. watches	_____	_____	**7.** newspapers		_____	_____
3. dictionaries	_____	_____	**8.** book bags		_____	_____
4. students	_____	_____	**9.** hats		_____	_____
5. erasers	_____	_____	**10.** doors		_____	_____

How many correct guesses did you make? _____

Who made the most correct guesses? _____

6 GENERAL KNOWLEDGE QUIZ

Work in pairs. Take turns. Ask each other these questions. Begin with **How many**. *(The answers are on page 221.)*

EXAMPLE:
A: How many people are there in China?

1. people/in China
   a. about 1,246,900,000   **b.** about 2,246,900,000   **c.** about 246,900,000

2. people/in Mexico
   a. about 80,294,000   **b.** about 102,026,000   **c.** about 90,294,000

3. members/of the United Nations
   a. about 200   **b.** about 100   **c.** about 300

4. planets/in the Solar System
   a. nine   **b.** ten   **c.** eight

5. players/on a soccer team
   a. eleven   **b.** ten   **c.** twelve

(continued on next page)

6. people/in Brazil
  a. about 173,790,000   **b.** about 120,790,000   **c.** about 100,790,000

7. people/in the United States
  a. about 175,000,000   **b.** about 375,000,000   **c.** about 275,000,000

8. continents/in the world
  a. seven   **b.** five   **c.** four

9. time zones/in the world
  a. twelve   **b.** four   **c.** twenty-four

10. players/on a baseball team
  a. ten   **b.** nine   **c.** twelve

Now ask your own question that begins with **How many**.

7 PEOPLE IN MY FAMILY   Grammar Notes 1–4

Work with a partner. Talk about people in your family. Use the quantifiers and nouns in the boxes.

Quantifiers

aren't any	a lot of	several
aren't many	many	some
		a few

Nouns

artists	princes/princesses	writers
athletes	detectives	teachers
comedians	soldiers	farmers
doctors	engineers	

EXAMPLE:
  A: Are there any comedians in your family?
  B: Well, my uncle Bob thinks he's a comedian. He always tells jokes. What about in your family?
  A: There aren't any comedians, but there are several artists. Two of my cousins and my aunt are artists.

8 CAN YOU COUNT THE BLOCKS?

How many blocks are there in this drawing?
Explain your answer to the class.

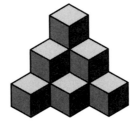

REVIEW OR SELFTEST

I. *Read each conversation. Circle the letter of the underlined word or group of words that is not correct.*

1. A: It's windy. Please <u>to open</u> the window.   **A B C D**
              _A

   B: Are you sure? <u>There's</u> <u>an air conditioner</u>. <u>Let's turn</u> it on.
                _B   _C   _D

2. A: <u>There are</u> <u>a lot of difficult words</u> in this article.   **A B C D**
         _A   _B

   B: <u>Are there</u> a dictionary <u>in the bookcase</u>?
        _C   _D

3. A: <u>There's</u> a note on the refrigerator. It says Aunt Valerie is   **A B C D**
        _A

    in the hospital.

   B: <u>Let's</u> <u>to send</u> <u>her</u> some flowers.
        _B   _C   _D

4. A: <u>How many</u> <u>women</u> <u>is there</u> in your class?   **A B C D**
        _A   _B   _C

   B: <u>There are</u> twelve including the teacher.
        _D

5. A: <u>Are you busy</u>?   **A B C D**
        _A

   B: <u>Me and John</u> are going to the computer lab. He's
        _B

    <u>showing me</u> how to use a new program. <u>Why don't you</u>
        _C   _D

    join us?

II. *Complete the questions.*

1. A: _____ teachers _____ there

    in your school?

   B: There are twenty.

2. A: _____ any soda machines in the building?

   B: Yes, there are.

3. A: _____ any malls near your apartment?

   B: No, there aren't.

4. A: _____ the teacher?

   B: Yes, she is.

(continued on next page)

5. A: _____ late?

   B: No, we aren't.

6. A: _____ chairs _____ there?

   B: There are six.

   A: _____ new chairs?

   B: No, they're not.

7. A: _____ a ladies' room on this floor?

   B: Yes, there is.

   A: _____ near the stairs?

   B: Yes, it is.

III. *Complete the paragraph. Choose the correct words.*

Doug's father is a businessman. _____ name is Pete. Doug's mother is
1. (He, Him, His)

a writer. _____ name is Elenore. Pete, Elenore, and Doug live in New York
2. (His, Her, Our)

City. _____ apartment is on the West Side. _____ a big
3. (They, Them, Their)   4. (It's, Its, They)

apartment. Many of _____ friends live near _____.
5. (they, them, their)   6. (they, them, their)

IV. *Look at this chart about the students in Al Brown's Level 2 English class. Write statements about the number of students from different countries. Use* **There is**, **There are**, *or* **There aren't** *and choose from the words in parentheses.*

English — Level 2	
Teacher: Al Brown	
Number of Students	**Country**
6	Korea
3	Thailand
1	Colombia

1. (a lot of, a few, one, any)   Korea

    There are a lot of students from Korea.

2. (a lot of, a few, one, any)   Thailand

_____

3. (a lot of, a few, one, any)   Colombia

_____

4. (a lot of, a few, one, any)   Turkey

_____

Now look at the chart and write questions. Use **How many**.

5. A: _____?

   B: Only one.

6. A: _____?

   B: A lot.

7. A: _____?

   B: A few.

8. A: _____ Germany?

   B: There aren't any.

V. *One sentence is correct. The other is wrong. Circle the correct sentence.*

1. a. They are thirteen students in my class.
   b. There are thirteen students in my class.

2. a. Give it to her.
   b. Give it to she.

3. a. He's a good scientist, but he's a bad science teacher.
   b. He's a good scientist, and he's a bad science teacher.

4. a. It is near we.
   b. It is near us.

5. a. There is three pens on the table.
   b. There are three pens on the table.

6. a. There aren't any restaurants near here.
   b. There aren't no restaurants near here.

VI. *Correct these sentences.*

1. The pot is hot. ~~You don't~~ Don't touch it!

2. Please you are quiet.

3. Why don't we to take a walk?

4. They's a young man at the door.

5. There aren't some books on the shelf.

6. There is several mistakes in your letter.

▶ *To check your answers, go to the Answer Key on page 221.*

From Grammar to Writing Sentence Combining with *And* and *But*

1 *Read these sentences. Then complete items 1 and 2.*

1. a. He's tall. He's a good basketball player.
   b. He's tall, **and** he's a good basketball player.

2. a. He's tall. He's a terrible basketball player.
   b. He's tall, **but** he's a terrible basketball player.

1. In number 1b
the word **and** _____.
   a. adds information
   b. adds a contrast

2. In number 2b
the word **but** _____.
   a. adds information
   b. adds a contrast

*Study this information about **and** and **but**.*

The Connectors *And* and *But*

1. We use connectors to help the reader understand our ideas more easily. Use **and** and **but** to connect two sentences.

And adds information to the idea in the first sentence.

But adds a contrast. This information is often surprising or unexpected.

- The book is good. It is easy to understand.

- The book is good, **and** it is easy to understand.
- The book is good, **but** it is difficult to understand.

---

2. When you use **and** or **but** to connect two sentences, use a comma before **and** or **but**.

- The house is big, **and** it has a lot of rooms.
- The house is big, **but** it has only one bathroom.

---

3. Don't use a comma to separate two descriptive adjectives.

- I am hungry **and** tired.
- He is tired **but** happy.

2 *Elenore and Pete Winston are talking about different apartments. Complete their conversation. Use* **and** *or* **but**.

ELENORE: It's difficult to find a good apartment in this city. Joe's apartment is cheap,

_____ it's far from stores. Our apartment is near stores, _____

it's expensive.

PETE: You're right. My uncle's apartment is cheap, _____ it's small. Dino's

apartment is big _____ cheap, _____ it's very dark.

ELENORE: Carol and Yoko are lucky. Their apartment is cheap _____

comfortable. It's near stores, _____ it's sunny, too.

PETE: They live in a small college town, _____ we live in a big city.

3 *Complete the sentences. Use* **and** *or* **but**.

1. She's friendly _____ popular.

2. She's friendly _____ unpopular.

3. The meeting is important, _____ few people are here.

4. The meeting is important, _____ many people are here.

5. Her last name is long, _____ it's hard to pronounce.

6. Her last name is long, _____ it's easy to pronounce.

4 *Draw a picture of your favorite city street. Then write a paragraph about the street. Use the connectors* **and** *and* **but** *in some of your sentences.*

OR

Compare stores in your neighborhood. Use the connectors **and** *and* **but** *in some of your sentences.*

EXAMPLE:
My favorite street is Edgehill Avenue in the Bronx. It is an unusual street. It is long and crooked. There are a lot of stores nearby, but there aren't any stores on Edgehill Avenue. There are only ten private houses. The houses are small and old. They are made of wood. The rooms are small, but the ceilings are high. There are many tall trees and beautiful gardens around the houses. The trees are very old. The people in the houses are old, too. I often go to Edgehill Avenue, and I know the street well because my grandparents live at 10 Edgehill Avenue.

REVIEW OR SELFTEST
ANSWER KEY

I.
1. A
2. C
3. C
4. C
5. B

II.
1. How many / are
2. Are there
3. Are there
4. Is she
5. Are we
6. How many / are
   Are they
7. Is there
   Is it

III.
1. His
2. Her
3. Their
4. It's
5. their
6. them

IV.
2. There are a few students from Thailand.
3. There is one student from Colombia.
4. There aren't any students from Turkey.
5. How many students are there from Colombia?
6. How many students are there from Korea?
7. How many students are there from Thailand?
8. How many students are there from Germany?

V.
1. b
2. a
3. a
4. b
5. b
6. a

VI.
2. Please be quiet.
3. Why don't we take a walk?
4. There's a young man at the door.
5. There are no books on the shelf.
6. There are several mistakes in your letter.

Answers to Exercise 6 on pages 213–214

1. a
2. b
3. a
4. a
5. a
6. a
7. c
8. a
9. c
10. b

Student B, you have a picture of a kitchen and a dining room. Answer your partner's questions about your picture.

Your partner has a picture of a living room and a bedroom. Ask your partner if the following items are in the living room or the bedroom. Write the name of the room (or rooms) they are in. Cross out items that are not in your partner's picture.

EXAMPLE:
B: Are there any lamps in the bedroom?
A: Yes, there are. There are two lamps in the bedroom.
B: Are there any lamps in the living room?
A: Yes, there's one lamp in the living room.

1. lamps _____ bedroom, living room _____

2. table _____

3. desk _____

4. sofa _____

5. TV _____

6. rug _____

7. plants _____

8. computer _____

9. VCR _____

10. books _____

11. bed _____

12. dresser _____

13. bookcase _____

14. mirror _____

APPENDICES

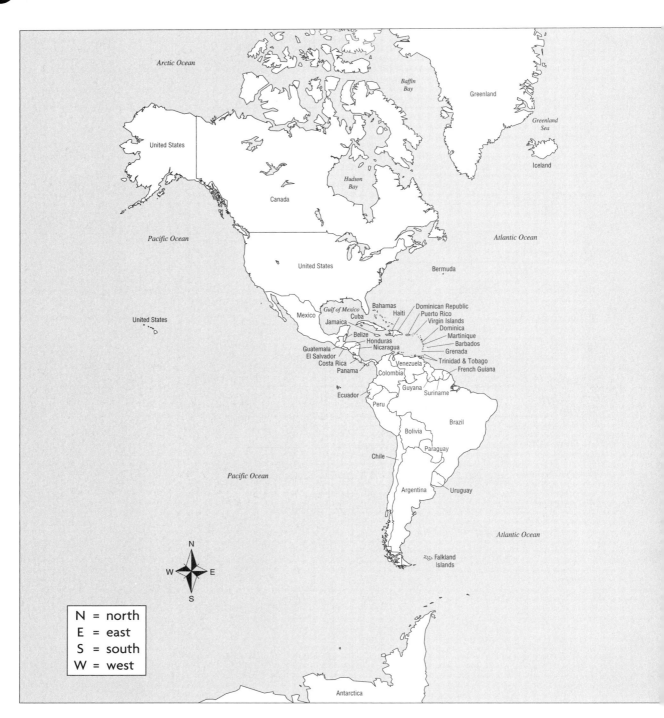

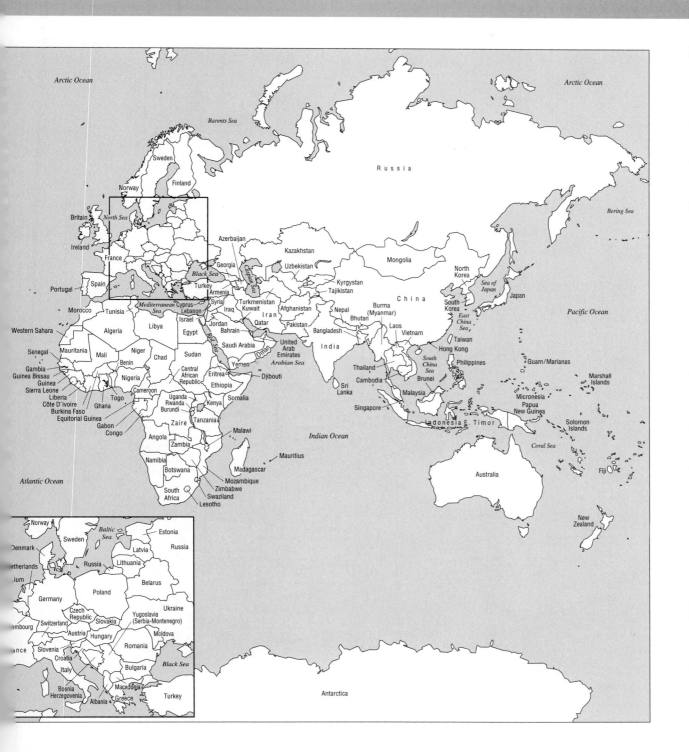

Arctic Ocean

Barents Sea

Sweden

Norway   Finland

Britain   North Sea

Ireland

France

Portugal   Spain

Russia

Bering Sea

Azerbaijan
Kazakhstan
Georgia   Uzbekistan   Mongolia   North
Black Sea   Caspian   Korea   Sea of
Turkey   Sea   Kyrgystan   China   South   Japan
Armenia   Tajikistan   Korea
Cyprus   Syria   Turkmenistan   Nepal   Burma   East   Japan
Mediterranean   Lebanon   Iraq   Kuwait   Afghanistan   (Myanmar)   China   Pacific Ocean
Sea   Israel   Iran   Bhutan   Sea
Morocco   Tunisia   Jordan   Bahrain   Pakistan   Laos   Taiwan
Western Sahara   Algeria   Libya   Egypt   Qatar   India   Bangladesh   Vietnam   Hong Kong
Saudi Arabia   United   South
Senegal   Mauritania   Niger   Chad   Sudan   Arab   Yemen   Arabian Sea   Thailand   China   Philippines   Guam/Marianas
Gambia   Mali   Emirates   Sea   Brunei   Marshall
Guinea Bissau   Benin   Nigeria   Central   Eritrea   Cambodia   Islands
Guinea   African   Ethiopia   Sri   Malaysia   Micronesia
Sierra Leone   Cameroon   Republic   Djibouti   Lanka   Papua
Liberia   Togo   Uganda   Somalia   Singapore   New Guinea
Côte D'ivoire   Ghana   Rwanda   Kenya   Indonesia E. Timor   Solomon
Burkina Faso   Gabon   Burundi   Tanzania   Islands
Equitorial Guinea   Congo   Zaire   Malawi   Indian Ocean   Coral Sea
Angola   Zambia   Mauritius   Fiji
Namibia   Botswana   Madagascar   Australia
Mozambique   New
South   Zimbabwe   Zealand
Africa   Swaziland
Lesotho

Atlantic Ocean

Antarctica

Norway
Baltic
Denmark   Sweden   Sea   Estonia
Russia
Netherlands   Russia   Latvia
Belgium   Lithuania
Germany   Poland   Belarus
Czech
Luxembourg   Republic   Slovakia   Ukraine
Switzerland   Austria   Hungary   Yugoslavia   Moldova
ance   Slovenia   (Serbia-Montenegro)
Croatia   Romania
Italy   Bulgaria   Black Sea
Bosnia   Macedonia
Herzegovina   Greece   Turkey
Albania

A-1

CARDINAL NUMBERS

1 = one	11 = eleven	21 = twenty-one
2 = two	12 = twelve	30 = thirty
3 = three	13 = thirteen	40 = forty
4 = four	14 = fourteen	50 = fifty
5 = five	15 = fifteen	60 = sixty
6 = six	16 = sixteen	70 = seventy
7 = seven	17 = seventeen	80 = eighty
8 = eight	18 = eighteen	90 = ninety
9 = nine	19 = nineteen	100 = one hundred
10 = ten	20 = twenty	200 = two hundred
		1,000 = one thousand
		1,000,000 = one million
		10,000,000 = ten million

EXAMPLES:

Cardinal Numbers

That book has seventy-seven pages.
There are thirty days in April.
There are six rows in the room.
She is twelve years old.
He has four children.

ORDINAL NUMBERS

1st = first	11th = eleventh	21st = twenty-first
2nd = second	12th = twelfth	30th = thirtieth
3rd = third	13th = thirteenth	40th = fortieth
4th = fourth	14th = fourteenth	50th = fiftieth
5th = fifth	15th = fifteenth	60th = sixtieth
6th = sixth	16th = sixteenth	70th = seventieth
7th = seventh	17th = seventeenth	80th = eightieth
8th = eighth	18th = eighteenth	90th = ninetieth
9th = ninth	19th = nineteenth	100th = one hundredth
10th = tenth	20th = twentieth	200th = two hundredth
		1,000th = one thousandth
		1,000,000th = one millionth
		10,000,000th = ten millionth

EXAMPLES:

Ordinal Numbers

It's his seventy-seventh birthday.
It's April thirtieth.
He's in the sixth row.
It's her twelfth birthday.
Bob is his first child. Mary is his second. John is his third, and Sue is his fourth.

TEMPERATURE

We measure the temperature in degrees (°).

Changing from degrees Fahrenheit to degrees Celsius:

$$(F° - 32) \times 5/9 = °C$$

Changing from degrees Celsius to degrees Fahrenheit:

$$(9/5 \times °C) + 32 = F°$$

DAYS OF THE WEEK

Weekdays	Weekend
Monday	Saturday
Tuesday	Sunday
Wednesday	
Thursday	
Friday	

MONTHS OF THE YEAR

Month	Abbreviation	Number of Days
January	Jan.	31
February	Feb.	28*
March	Mar.	31
April	Apr.	30
May	May	31
June	Jun.	30
July	Jul.	31
August	Aug.	31
September	Sept.	30
October	Oct.	31
November	Nov.	30
December	Dec.	31

*February has 29 days in a leap year, every four years.

THE SEASONS	TITLES

THE SEASONS

Spring—March 21st–June 20th

Summer—June 21st–September 20th

Autumn or Fall—September 21st–December 20th

Winter—December 21st-March 20th

TITLES

Mr. (Mister) / mɪstər / unmarried or married man

Ms. / mɪz /   unmarried or married woman

Miss. / mɪs /   unmarried woman

Mrs. / mɪsɪz /   married woman

Dr. (Doctor) / daktər / doctor (medical doctor or Ph.D.)

❹ Time

It's one o'clock.
(It's 1:00.)

It's five after one.
(It's 1:05.)

It's one-ten.
It's ten after one.
(It's 1:10.)

It's one-fifteen.
It's a quarter after one.
(It's 1:15.)

It's one twenty-five.
It's twenty-five after one.
(It's 1:25.)

It's one-thirty.
It's half past one.
(It's 1:30.)

It's one forty-five.
It's a quarter to two.
(It's 1:45.)

It's one-fifty.
It's ten to two.
(It's 1:50.)

TALKING ABOUT TIME

1. You can ask about time this way:

- **A: What time is it?**
- **B:** It's one o'clock.

2. **A.M.** means before noon
(the hours between midnight and noon).

- It's 10:00 **A.M.**

P.M. means after noon
(the hours between noon and midnight).

- It's 10:00 **P.M.**

BE CAREFUL! When people say 12:00 A.M.,
they mean midnight. When people say
12:00 P.M., they mean noon.

3. We often write time with numbers.

- It's one o'clock = It's **1:00**.
- It's two-twenty = It's **2:20**.

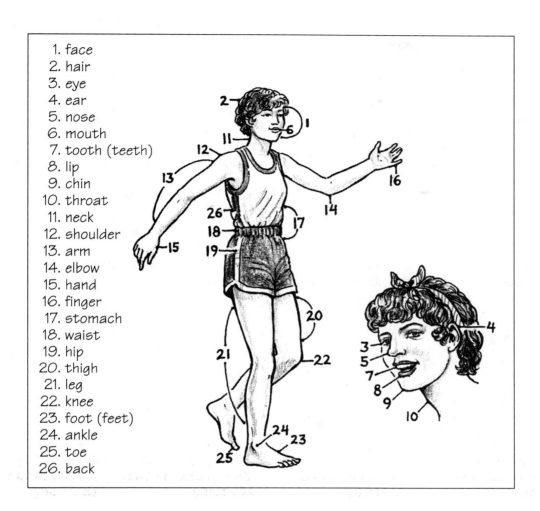

1. face
2. hair
3. eye
4. ear
5. nose
6. mouth
7. tooth (teeth)
8. lip
9. chin
10. throat
11. neck
12. shoulder
13. arm
14. elbow
15. hand
16. finger
17. stomach
18. waist
19. hip
20. thigh
21. leg
22. knee
23. foot (feet)
24. ankle
25. toe
26. back

Medical Problems

I have a backache.
I have an earache.
I have a headache.
I have a sore throat.
I have a stomachache. (I'm nauseous; I have diarrhea; I'm constipated.)
I have a fever.
My nose is running.
I have a cough.
I have a pain in my back.
My neck hurts.

U.S. Holidays (Federal and Legal Holidays and Other Special Days)

January

*New Year's Day	January 1st
*Martin Luther King, Jr.'s Birthday	January 15th (observed on the closest Monday)

February

Valentine's Day	February 14th
*George Washington's Birthday	February 22nd (observed on the closest Monday)

March

April

April Fools' Day	April 1st

May

Mother's Day	the second Sunday in May
*Memorial Day	May 30th (observed on the last Monday in May)

June

Flag Day	June 14th
Father's Day	the third Sunday in June

July

*Independence Day	July 4th

August

September

*Labor Day	the first Monday in September

October

*Columbus Day	October 12th (observed on the closest Monday)
Halloween	October 31st

November

Election Day	the first Tuesday after the first Monday in November
*Veterans' Day	November 11th
*Thanksgiving	the fourth Thursday in November

December

*Christmas	December 25th
New Year's Eve	December 31st

*federal legal holidays

Canadian Holidays (Legal and Public Holidays)

January

New Year's Day	January 1st
Sir John A. Macdonald's Birthday	January 11th

February

Valentine's Day	February 14th

March

*St. Patrick's Day	the Monday nearest March 17th

March or April

*Good Friday	
*Easter Monday	

April

April Fool's Day	April 1st

May

Mother's Day	the second Sunday in May
Victoria Day	the Monday preceding May 25th

June

Father's Day	the third Sunday in June

St. John the Baptist's Day	the Monday nearest June 24th (only in Quebec)

July

Canada Day	July 1st

August

Civic Holiday	the first Monday in August (celebrated in several provinces)
Discovery Day	the third Monday in August (only in the Yukon)

September

Labor Day	the first Monday in September

October

Thanksgiving Day	the second Monday in October
Halloween	October 31st

November

Remembrance Day	November 11th

December

Christmas Day	December 25th
Boxing Day	December 26th

*Many Americans in the United States observe these religious holidays too. However, these days are not official U.S. holidays.

SPELLING RULES

1. Add *-s* to form the plural of most nouns.

- student—students
- picture—pictures
- chief—chiefs

2. Add *-es* to form the plural of nouns that end in *ss*, *ch*, *sh*, and *x*. (This ending adds another syllable.)

- class—classes
- watch—watches
- dish—dishes
- box—boxes

3. Add *-es* to form the plural of nouns that end in *o* preceded by a consonant.

- potato—potatoes

EXCEPTION: Add *s* to plural nouns ending in *o* that refer to music.

- piano—pianos
- soprano—sopranos

4. Add *-s* to form the plural of nouns that end in *o* preceded by a vowel.

- radio—radios

5. To form the plural of words that end in *y* preceded by a consonant, change the *y* to *i* and add *-es*.

- dictionary—dictionaries
- fly—flies

6. To form the plural of words that end in *y* preceded by a vowel, add *-s*.

- boy—boys
- day—days

7. To form the plural of certain nouns that end in *f* or *fe*, change the *f* to *v* and add *-es*.

- half—halves
- loaf—loaves
- knife—knives
- wife—wives

8. Some plural nouns are irregular.

- woman—women
- child—children
- person—people
- mother-in-law—mothers-in-law
- man—men
- foot—feet
- tooth—teeth

9. Some nouns do not have a singular form.

- (eye) glasses
- clothes
- pants
- scissors

10. Some plural nouns are the same as the singular noun.

- Chinese—Chinese
- fish—fish
- sheep—sheep

PRONUNCIATION RULES

1. The final sounds for regular plural nouns are / s /, / z /, and / ɪz /.	
2. The plural is pronounced /s/ after the voiceless sounds / p /, / t /, k /, / f /, and / θ /.	• cups • works • myths • hats • cuffs
3. The plural is pronounced /z/ after the voiced sounds / b /, / d /, / g /, / v /, / m /, / n /, / ŋ /, / l /, / r /, and / ð /.	• crabs • cards • rugs
4. The plural *s* is pronounced / z / after all vowel sounds.	• day—days • toe—toes
5. The plural *s* is pronounced / ɪz / after the sounds / s /, / z /, / ʃ /, / ʒ /, / ʧ /, and / ʤ /.(This adds another syllable to the word.)	• races • dishes • causes

8 Possessive Nouns

1. Add **'s** to form the possessive of singular nouns.	• Lulu**'s** last name is Winston.
2. To form the possessive of plural nouns ending in *s*, add only an apostrophe (**'**).	• The girl**s'** gym is on this floor. • The boy**s'** locker room is across the hall.
3. In hyphenated words (*mother-in-law, father-in-law*, etc.) and in phrases showing joint possession, only the last word is possessive in form.	• My sister-in-law**'s** apartment is big. • Elenore and Pete**'s** apartment is comfortable.
4. To form the possessive of plural nouns that do not end in *s*, add **'s**.	• The men**'s** room is next to the water fountain.
5. To form the possessive of one-syllable singular nouns that end in *s*, add **'s**. To form the possessive of words of more than one syllable that end in *s*, add an **'** or an **'s**.	• **James's** apartment is beautiful. • **McCullers's** novels are interesting. OR • **McCullers'** novels are interesting.
6. **BE CAREFUL!** Don't confuse possessive nouns with the contraction of the verb *be*.	• **Carol's** a student. = **Carol** *is* a student. • **Carol's** book is open. = **Her** book is open.

Common Non-count Nouns*

Liquids	Food	Too small to count	School subjects
milk	bread	sugar	math
coffee	cheese	salt	history
oil	lettuce	pepper	geography
juice	broccoli	cinnamon	biology
soda	ice cream	rice	chemistry
water	butter	sand	music
beer	mayon-	baking powder	
	naise	cereal	
	ketchup	spaghetti	
	jam	wheat	
	jelly	corn	
	fish		
	meat		
	sour cream		
	soup		

City problems	Weather	Gases	Abstract ideas	Others
traffic	snow	oxygen	love	money
pollution	rain	carbon dioxide	beauty	mail
crime	ice	nitrogen	happiness	furniture
	fog	air	luck	homework
			advice	information
			help	jewelry
			noise	garbage
			time	toothpaste
				paper

*Some nouns can be either count or non-count nouns.

I'd like some **chicken**. (non-count)
There were three **chickens** in the yard. (count)

Did you eat any **cake**? (non-count)
I bought a **cake** at the bakery. (count)

Common Containers, Measure Words, and Portions

a bottle of (milk, soda, catsup)
a bowl of (cereal, soup, rice)
a can of (soda, beans, tuna fish)
a cup of (hot chocolate, coffee, tea)
a foot of (snow, water)
a gallon of (juice, gas, paint)
a head of (lettuce)
an inch of (snow, rain)
a loaf of (bread)

a pair of (pants, skis, gloves)
a piece of (paper, cake, pie)
a pint of (ice cream, cream)
a quart of (milk)
a roll of (film, toilet paper, paper towels)
a slice of (toast, cheese, meat)
a tablespoon of (flour, sugar, baking soda)
a teaspoon of (sugar, salt, pepper)
a tube of (toothpaste, glue)

1. *The* is the definite article. You can use *the* before singular count nouns, plural count nouns, and non-count nouns.

- **The** hat is red.
- **The** hats are red.
- **The** coffee is hot.

2. Use *the* for specific things that the listener and speaker know about.

- **A:** How was **the** test?
- **B:** It was easy.

- **A:** Would you like to read **the** paper?
- **B:** Yes, thanks.

3. Use *the* when the speaker and listener know there is only one of the item.

- **A:** Is there a cafeteria in this school?
- **B:** Yes, **the** cafeteria is on the third floor.

4. Use *the* when you are talking about part of a group.

- Meat is usually expensive, but **the** meat at Ron's Butcher Shop is cheap and delicious.

5. Use *the* when you talk about something for the second time.

- **A:** What did you buy?
- **B:** Some apples and some pears. **The** apples were bad, but **the** pears were delicious.

6. Use *the* before the plural name of a whole family.

- **The** Winstons live in New York City.

7. Use *the* before the names of oceans, rivers, mountain ranges, seas, canals, deserts, and zoos.

- **The Pacific Ocean** is on the West Coast.
- **The Mississippi River** is the longest river in the United States.
- We visited **the Rocky Mountains.**
- Where is **the Dead Sea**?
- The boat went through **the Suez Canal**.
- **The Sahara Desert** is growing.
- We visited **the San Diego Zoo.**

8. Use *the* with phrases with *of* when there is only one of the item that follows *the*.

- Paris is **the capital of France**.
- I attended **the University of Michigan**.
  BUT
- He drank **a** cup of tea.

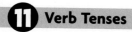

THE PRESENT TENSE OF *BE*

SINGULAR		
SUBJECT	**BE**	
I	**am**	
You	**are**	a student.
He She	**is**	
It	**is**	in the United States.

PLURAL		
SUBJECT	**BE**	
We You They	**are**	in the United States.

THE PAST TENSE OF *BE*

SINGULAR			
SUBJECT	**BE**		**TIME MARKER**
I	**was**		
You	**were**	at a restaurant	last night.
He She It	**was**		

PLURAL			
SUBJECT	**BE**		**TIME MARKER**
We You They	**were**	at a restaurant	last night.

THE PRESENT PROGRESSIVE

SUBJECT	**BE**	**BASE FORM OF VERB + -ING**
I	**am**	
You	**are**	
He She It	**is**	working.
We You They	**are**	

THE SIMPLE PRESENT TENSE

SUBJECT	VERB
I You We They	**work.**
He She It	**works.**

THE SIMPLE PAST TENSE

SUBJECT	BASE FORM OF VERB + -ED / -D / -IED
I You He She It We You They	**worked.** **arrived.** **cried.**

THE PAST PROGRESSIVE

SUBJECT	PAST TENSE OF *BE*	BASE FORM OF VERB + *-ING*
I He She It	**was**	working.
We You They	**were**	

WILL FOR THE FUTURE

SUBJECT	*WILL*	BASE FORM OF VERB	
I You He She It We You They	**will**	**work**	tomorrow.

BE GOING TO FOR THE FUTURE

SUBJECT	*BE*	*GOING TO*	BASE FORM OF VERB	
I	**am**			
You	**are**			
He She	**is**	**going to**	**work**	tomorrow.
You We They	**are**			
It	**is**	**going to**	**rain**	tomorrow.

12 Base Forms and Past-Tense Forms of Common Irregular Verbs

Base form	Past-tense form	Base form	Past-tense form	Base form	Past-tense form
become	became	go	went	sell	sold
begin	began	grow	grew	send	sent
bite	bit	hang	hung	shake	shook
blow	blew	have	had	shoot	shot
break	broke	hear	heard	shut	shut
bring	brought	hide	hid	sing	sang
build	built	hit	hit	sit	sat
buy	bought	hold	held	sleep	slept
catch	caught	hurt	hurt	speak	spoke
choose	chose	keep	kept	spend	spent
come	came	know	knew	stand	stood
cost	cost	lead	led	steal	stole
do	did	leave	left	swim	swam
draw	drew	lend	lent	take	took
drink	drank	lose	lost	teach	taught
drive	drove	make	made	tear	tore
eat	ate	meet	met	tell	told
fall	fell	pay	paid	think	thought
feed	fed	put	put	throw	threw
feel	felt	quit	quit	understand	understood
fight	fought	read*	read*	wake	woke
find	found	ride	rode	wear	wore
fly	flew	ring	rang	win	won
forget	forgot	run	ran	write	wrote
get	got	say	said		
give	gave	see	saw		

*Pronounce the base form / rɪd /. Pronounce the past-tense form / rɛd /.

13 The Present Progressive: Spelling Rules

1. Add -*ing* to base form of the verb.

- drink—drink**ing**
- eat—eat**ing**
- see—see**ing**

2. If a verb ends in a silent *e*, drop the final *e* and add -*ing*.

- smile—smil**ing**

3. If a one-syllable verb ends in a consonant, a vowel, and a consonant (CVC), double the last consonant before adding -*ing*.

   However, do not double the last consonant if it is a *w*, *x*, or *y*.

CVC ↓↓↓
sit—sit**ting**

CVC ↓↓↓
run—run**ning**

- sew—sew**ing**
- mix—mix**ing**

- play—play**ing**

4. In two-syllable words that end in a consonant, a vowel, and a consonant (CVC), double the last consonant only if the last syllable is stressed.

- admit—admi**tt**ing (last syllable is stressed)
- whisper—whispe**r**ing (last syllable is not stressed)

SPELLING RULES FOR THE THIRD-PERSON SINGULAR AFFIRMATIVE

1. Add **-s** to form the third-person singular of most verbs.

- Pete works. I work too.
- Doug wears sweatshirts. I wear shirts.

Add **-es** to words that end in **ch**, **s**, **sh**, **x**, or **z**.

- Norma teaches Spanish. I teach English.
- Lulu washes her cloths on Tuesday. Elenore and Pete wash their clothes on Sunday.

2. When a base-form verb ends in a consonant + **y**, change the **y** to **i** and add **-es**.

- I study at home. Carol studies at the library.

Do not change the **y** when the base form ends in a vowel + **y**. Add **-s**.

- Dan plays tennis. I play tennis, too.

3. Some verbs have irregular forms for the third-person singular.

- I have   He **has**.
- I do.   She **does**.
- I go.   It **goes**.

PRONUNCIATION RULES FOR THE THIRD-PERSON SINGULAR AFFIRMATIVE

1. The final sound for the third-person singular form of the simple present tense is pronounced / s /, / z /, or / ɪz /. The final sounds of the third-person singular are the same as the final sounds of plural nouns. See Appendix 7 on pages A-7 and A-8.

/ s /	/ z /	/ ɪz /
talks	loves	dances

2. **Do** and **say** have a change in vowel sound.

- I say. / seɪ /
- I do. / du/

- He says. / sɛz /
- He does. / dʌz /

SPELLING RULES

1. If the verb ends in an **e**, add **-d**.

   • arrive—arrive**d**   • like—like**d**

2. If the verb ends in a consonant, add **-ed**.

   • rain—rain**ed**   • help—help**ed**

3. If a one-syllable verb ends in a consonant, a vowel, and a consonant (CVC), double the last consonant and add **-ed**.

   CVC   **CVC**

   hug—hu**gged**   rub—ru**bbed**

   However, do not double the last consonant if it is a **w**, **x**, or **y**.

   • bow—bowed   • play—played
   • mix—mixed

4. If a two-syllable verb ends in a consonant, a vowel, and a consonant (CVC), double the last consonant only if the last syllable is stressed.

   • refér—refer**r**ed (the last syllable is stressed)
   • énter—enter**ed** (the last syllable is not stressed)

5. If the verb ends in a consonant + **y**, change the **y** to **i** and add **-ed**.

   • worry—worr**ied**   • carry—carr**ied**

6. If the verb ends in a vowel + **y**, do not change the **y** to **i**. Add **-ed**.

   • play—play**ed**
   • annoy—anno**yed**

   EXCEPTIONS: *pay—paid, lay—laid, say—said*

PRONUNCIATION RULES

1. The final sounds for regular verbs in the past tense are $/t/$, $/d/$, and $/\text{ɪd}/$.

2. The plural is pronounced /s/ after the voiceless sounds $/f/$, $/k/$, $/p/$, $/s/$, $/\text{ʧ}/$, and $/ʃ/$.

   • laughed   • missed   • wished
   • licked   • watched   • sipped

3. The final sound is pronounced $/d/$ after the voiced sounds $/b/$, $/g/$, $/\text{ʤ}/$, $/l/$, $/m/$, $/n/$, $/r/$, $/ŋ/$, $/ð/$, $/ʒ/$, $/v/$, and $/z/$.

   • rubbed   • hummed   • bathed
   • hugged   • banned   • massaged
   • judged   • occurred   • lived
   • pulled   • banged   • surprised

4. The final sound is pronounced $/d/$ after vowel sounds

   • played   • tied   • argued
   • skied   • snowed

5. The final sound is pronounced $/\text{ɪd}/$ after $/t/$ and $/d/$. $/\text{ɪd}/$ adds a syllable to the verb.

   • want—wanted   • instruct—instructed
   • rest—rested   • attend—attended

	COMPARATIVE FORM (USED TO COMPARE TWO PEOPLE, PLACES, OR THINGS)			
Sally	is	**older** **busier** **more industrious**	**than**	her sister.
	types	**faster** **more quickly**		

	SUPERLATIVE FORM (USED TO COMPARE THREE OR MORE PEOPLE, PLACES, OR THINGS)		
Sally	is	**oldest** **busiest** **most industrious**	of the three.
	types	**the** **fastest** **most quickly**	

	EQUATIVE FORM (USED TO SHOW THAT TWO PEOPLE, PLACES, OR THINGS ARE THE SAME)			
Sally	is	**as** **tall** **busy** **industrious**	**as**	Bob.
	types	**fast** **quickly**		

FUNCTION	MODALS	EXAMPLES
to make polite requests	**would like** **May I . . .** **Can I . . .** **Would you (please)** **Could you (please)**	I**'d like** to buy a gold bracelet. **May I** help you? **Can I** please see your paper? **Would you** please lend me your pen? **Could you** please help me?
to express possibility (present or future)	**may** **might**	Take an umbrella. It **may** rain. We **might** visit my cousin this evening.
to express future possibility	**can** **could**	How **can** I get to the library? You **could** go by bus or by train.
to talk about the future	**will**	He **will** be three years old next week.
to express present ability	**can**	I **can** type fifty words a minute.
to express past ability	**could**	I **could** run very fast ten years ago.
to express necessity in the present or future	**must** **have to**	You **must** pay the rent by the first of the month. She **has to** work today.
to express past necessity	**had to**	We **had to** read two new chapters for today.
to express advisability	**should** **ought to** **had better**	He **should** see a doctor. He doesn't sound very good. We **ought to** study today. They**'d better** return my money.
to promise or assure	**will**	I**'ll be** there at 10.
to express strong prohibition	**mustn't**	You **mustn't** smoke near the chemical factory.
to indicate that something is not a requirement	**don't / doesn't have to**	You **don't have to** type your composition. She **doesn't have to** wear a suit at her office.

These are the pronunciation symbols used in this text. Listen to the pronunciation of the key words.

VOWELS		CONSONANTS			
Symbol	**Key Word**	**Symbol**	**Key Word**	**Symbol**	**Key Word**
i	beat, feed	p	pack, happy	ʃ	ship, machine, station,
ɪ	bit, did	b	back, rubber		special, discussion
eɪ	date, paid	t	tie	ʒ	measure, vision
ɛ	bet, bed	d	die	h	hot, who
æ	bat, bad	k	came, key, quick	m	men
ɑ	box, odd, father	g	game, guest	n	sun, know, pneumonia
ɔ	bought, dog	tʃ	church, nature, watch	ŋ	sung, ringing
oʊ	boat, road	dʒ	judge, general, major	w	wet, white
ʊ	book, good	f	fan, photograph	l	light, long
u	boot, food, student	v	van	r	right, wrong
ʌ	but, mud, mother	θ	thing, breath	y	yes, use, music
ə	banana, among	ð	then, breathe		
ɚ	shirt, murder	s	sip, city, psychology		
aɪ	bite, cry, buy, eye	z	zip, please, goes		
aʊ	about, how				
ɔɪ	voice, boy				
ɪr	deer				
ɛr	bare				
ɑr	bar				
ɔr	door				
ʊr	tour				

INDEX

This index is for the full and split editions. All entries are in the full book. Page numbers for Volume A of the split edition are in black. Page numbers for Volume B are in color.

A / an, 41-42, 309-310
  one in place of, 138
Ability
  can / could for, 328-329
Adjectives
  as plus adjective / adverb, 377, 379, **A16**
  before nouns, 397-398
  comparative form of, 362-364, **A16**
  demonstrative adjectives, *this / that / these / those*, 132
  descriptive, 46-50
  equative form, 377-379, **A16**
  irregular comparative form of, 362-364
  one of the plus superlative, 425
  one / ones after, 138
  order of before nouns, 397-398
  plus *enough*, 377-378
  possessive, 78-84, 250
  superlative form of, 424-425, **A16**
  too plus adjective, 377-378
  very plus adjective, 377, 379
Adverbs
  comparative form of, 370-372, **A16**
  equative form, 377-379≈
  frequency, adverbs of, 228-230
  irregular comparative form of, 370-372
  of manner, 370-372
  superlative form of, 424-425, **A16**
Advice
  with *had better*, 404-406, **A17**
  with *should*, 403-405, **A17**
A few / a little, 210, 309, 311

A little, 309, 311
A lot of / lots of, 210, 309
  with non-count nouns, 311
Alphabet, 1
And, use of, 219-220
  comma rules, 102
Any, 203, 309-310, 317-318
Apostrophe, punctuation rules, 7, 80, 102
Are there / is there, 202
Articles
  a / an (indefinite), 41-42, 309-310
  the (definite article), 42, **A10**
  there is / there are with, 210
As
  plus adjective / adverb, 377-379
  same plus, 377-379

Badly, 372
Be
  adverbs of frequency after the verb, 230
  affirmative statements, 6-7, 28-29, 263-264, **A11**
  contractions with affirmative statements, 6-7, 28-29
  contractions with negative statements, 13,18, 28-29, 263-264
  negative statements, 13,18, 28-29, 56, 263-264
  as a non-action verb, 237
  past tense, 27-32, 160, **A11**
  present progressive, 56, **A11**
  present tense, 7, 20-21, **A11**
  questions with, 20-21
  subject pronouns, contractions with, 7, 13
  wh- questions

  past tense with, 271
  present tense with, 72
  yes / no questions
    past tense with, 28, 263-264
    present tense with, 20-21
Be going to, for the future, 279-282, **A12**
  probably with, 281
Behind, 52
Better, 362
Between, 52
Body, parts of, **A5**
Born, 272
Business letter, writing a, 355-356
But, use of, 219-220

Can / could
  ability and possibility, used for, 328-329, **A17**
  polite requests; *can I, may I, could I* for, 328-329, **A17**
Can I, 328-329, **A17**
Can't, 328-329
Capital letters, 35-36
Cardinal numbers, 87, **A3**
Comma, 102
Comparative form
  adjectives, 362-364, **A16**
    irregular, 362-364
  adverbs, 370-372, **A16**
    irregular, 370-372
  more, use of, 364
  much, use of, 364
  than, use of, 363
Comparisons, *See* Comparative form, Equative form, Superlative form. *See also* Adjectives, Adverbs
Conjunctions
  and, 219-220

but, 219-220
Connectors
  and / *but*, 219-220
  time words, 148
Containers, common, A9
Contractions
  affirmative statements, 6-7, 9, 109-110, 263-264
  be
    affirmative statements, 6-7, 9, 263-264
    negative statements, 13, 28
    subject pronouns, contractions with, 7, 13
  can / *could*, 328-329
  defined, 7
  desires, 343-344
  didn't, 264
  do not / *does not*, 415-417
  had better, 404, 406, A17
  let's, 184-187
  must not, 416-417
  negative statements, 13,18, 28-29
  past tense with, 28-29
  present progressive, 56-57
  short answers and use of, 21
  shouldn't, use of, 403-405
  simple present tense and, 109-110
  singular nouns and, 7
  subject pronouns with, 7, 13
  there is / *there are*, 202-203
  use of, 7, 13
  wasn't / *weren't*, 160, 264
  wh- questions with, 72
  will, 291, 293
Could I, 328-329, A17
Could you please, 343-344, A17
Count nouns, 309-311
  a / *an*, 41-42
  a lot of / *lots of*, 210
  common non-count, A9
  one / *ones*, use of, 137-138
  use of enough before, 319

Days of the week, A3
Definite article
  the, 309-310, A10

uses of, A10
Demonstrative adjectives and pronouns, *this* / *that* / *these* / *those*, 132
Descriptive adjectives, 47
Desires
  would like, 343-344, A17
Didn't, 263-264
Different from, 378-379
Direct objects, 194-195
Dislike, 245
Do not / *does not have to*, 415-417, A17
Don't have to, 415-417, A17

Enough
  adjective plus, 377-378
  infinitive after, 377-378
  plus noun, 317, 319
Equative form of adjectives and adverbs, 377-379, A16
Exclamation point, 179
Expressions of frequency, 229

Farther, 362
Finally, 145
Finish, 244-245
First, 145
Frequency
  adverbs of, 228-230
  be, adverbs of frequency after the verb, 230
  expressions of, 229
  questions of, 228
  time markers, 28, 229
Future
  be going to for, 279-282, A12
  present progressive for, 282
  time markers, 28, 280, 282
  wh- questions, 280, 343
  will for the future, 291-293, A12, A17
  yes / *no* questions, 279-282

Gerunds, 244-245

Had better
  advice, used for, 406, A17
  forms of, 404
Had to, 417, A17

Hard / *hardly*, 372
Hate, 245
Have, 110
Have to
  forms of, 415-416
  necessity, used for, 417, A17
  past tense, 417
Holidays, 90-91, A6
  Canada, in, A6
  United States, in, A6
How long, 167
How many, 209-210, 317-318
How much, 317-318
How often, 228-230
Hyphenated words, possessive nouns and, A8
Hyphen, use of, rules, 179

Imperatives, 186-187
In, 52
Indefinite articles,
  A / *an*, 41-42, 309-310
  uses of, 309-310
Indirect objects, 194-195
Infinitive, 244-245
  after adjective plus *enough* or *too*, 378
  verbs followed by, 244-245
  would you like plus, 343-344
Invitations and offers, 343-344
Irregular verbs, past tense of, 160, A13
Is there / *are there*, 201-207
It / *its*
  it's versus, 80
  one / *ones and*, 138
  in place of a possessive pronoun, 138
  this / *that* and, 138

Less, with adjectives, 364
Let's, 186-187
Linking verbs, 372

Many / *much*, 210, 309, 311
Maps
  United States and Canada, A2
  world, the, A0–A1
May, 336, A17
May I, 328-329, A17

Measure words, A9
Might, 336, **A17**
Modals
   can / could, 328-329, **A17**
   can I, 328-329, **A17**
   could I, 328-329, **A17**
   could you please, 343-344,
     A17
   described, 328
   don't / doesn't have to,
     415-417, **A17**
   had better, 404, 406, **A17**
   had to, 417, **A17**
   have to, 415-417, **A17**
   may I, 328-329, **A17**
   may / might for possibility,
     336, **A17**
   must, 416-417, **A17**
   mustn't, 416-417, **A17**
   ought to, 405, **A17**
   should, 403-405, **A17**
   would you please, 343-344,
     A17
Months of the year, A3
More, comparisons with,
   363-364, **A16**
Most, superlative with,
   424-425, **A16**
Much, comparisons with, 364
Much to, 378
Must, 416-417, **A17**
Mustn't, 416-417, **A17**

Near, 52
Necessity
   have to, 415-417, **A17**
   must, 415-417, **A17**
Negative questions, 263-264
Next to, 52
Non-action verbs
   simple present tense with, 110
   used as action verbs, 237
   use of, 236-237
Non-count nouns, 309-311
   common, A9
Noun phrase, *one* in place of,
   138
Nouns
   a / an + count, 41-42
   count, 309-311

non-count, 309-311, A9
plus verbs, 242-248
proper, 42
Numbers
   cardinal, 87, A3
   how many, use in answers to,
     209
   hyphen rules, 179
   ordinal, 86-87, A3
   quantifiers and, 209
   there is / there are, with, 210

Object pronouns, 194-195
Objects
   direct and indirect, 194-195
On, 52
One of the, superlative
   adjective plus, 425
One / ones, 136-137
   it and, 138
Opinion, expressing and
   supporting, 437-439
Ordinal numbers, 86-87, A3
Ought to
   should and, 405, **A17**

Past continuous. *See* Past
   progressive
Past progressive
   affirmative statements,
     386-387, **A12**
   interrupted action, with,
     386-387
   negative statements, 386-387
   short answers, 386
   wh- questions, 386
   yes / no questions, 386
Past tense
   be, 28-29
     affirmative statements,
      28, **A11**
     negative statements, 28
     wh- questions, 271
     yes / no questions, 28
   had to, 417, **A17**
   have to, 415-417, **A17**
   irregular verbs, common,
     160, **A13**
   See also Simple Past Tense
Past time markers, 29

Period, punctuation rules, 103
Permission
   may for, 336, **A17**
Phrases
   with gerunds, 245
Plural nouns
   pronunciation rules, A8
   spelling rules, A7
Polite requests
   can I, 328-329, **A17**
   could I, 328-329, **A17**
   could you please, 343, **A17**
   may I, 328-329, **A17**
   short answers to, 328
   would you please, 343–344,
     A17
Possessive adjectives, 79-80,
   250
Possessive nouns
   contraction of verb *be*
     distinguished from, A8
   hyphenated words and, A8
   it in place of, 138
   questions with *whose* and,
     79-80
   singular and plural nouns,
     forming possessive of, A8
Possessive pronouns, 79-80,
   250
Possibility
   can / could used for, 328-329,
     A17
   may / might for, 336, **A17**
Prefer, 245
Prepositional phrases
   be with, 7
   superlatives and, 426
Prepositions
   of place, 52
   of time and questions with
     when / what, 86-87
Present affirmative statements
   of *be*, 6-7, **A11**
   contractions, 6-7, 28-29
   past tense of, 28-29, **A11**
   present tense of, 7, **A11**
Present continuous. *See*
   Present progressive
Present negative statements of
   be

contractions, 13, 28-29
  past tense of *be*, 28-29
  present progressive, 56
Present progressive, 56-57,
  94-95
  affirmative statements, 56, A11
  answers to *yes / no*
    questions, 56
  contractions and, 56
  contractions in answers, 56
  for future, 282
  negative statements, 56
  non-action verbs and use
    of, 237
  short answers and, 56
  simple present tense and,
    228-229
  spelling rules, A13
  wh- questions, 94-95
  yes / no questions and, 56
Probably
  be going to the future with,
    281
  will for the future with, 293
Pronouns
  contractions with subject,
    7, 13
  direct and indirect objects,
    with, 194-195
  object pronouns, 195
  possessive, 250
  subject pronouns, 6, 194
    contractions with, 7, 13
Pronunciation rules
  consonants, A18
  plural nouns, A8
  simple past tense of regular
    verbs, A15
  simple present tense, A14
  vowels, A18
Proper nouns, 42
Punctuation rules
  apostrophe, 7, 80, 102
  comma, 102
  exclamation point, 179
  hyphen, 179
  period, 103
  question mark, 103
  quotation marks, 180

Quantifiers, 209-210, 309-311
  count and non-count nouns,
    with, 317-319
  how many, use in answers to,
    209-210
  negative statements with, 209
  numbers and, 209
Question mark, punctuation
  rules for, 103
Questions
  are there, 209
  frequency, 228-229
  how long, 167
  how many / much, 209-210,
    317-319
  how often, 228-229
  negative, 263-264
  present progressive, 56,
    92-99
  simple past tense and *wh-*,
    165-175, 271-272
  simple past tense and *yes /
    no*, 263-264
  simple present tense and
    wh-, 122-130
  what, 71-72, 86-87, 94-95
  when, 86-87
  where, 71-72
  who, 71-72, 94-95
  whom, 94-95
  whose, 79-80
  why, 94-95
  See also *Yes / no* questions
Quotation marks, punctuation
  rules, 180

Refuse, 245
Requests
  could you please, 343, A17
  would you please, 343, A17

Same
  as, 377-379
  plus noun, 377-379
Seasons, the, A4
Several, 309
Should
  affirmative statements with,
    403, 405, A17
  negative statements, 403, 405

  ought to and, 405, A17
  short answers, 403
  wh- questions, 403-404
  yes / no questions with, 404
Simple past tense
  irregular verbs, affirmative
    and negative statements,
    160
  pronunciation rules of
    regular verbs, A15
  regular verbs, affirmative
    and negative statements,
    151-152
  review of, 263-264
  spelling rules of regular
    verbs, A15
  time markers, 29-30, 151-152
  wh- questions, 167-169,
    263-264
  yes / no questions, 167-169
  See also Past Tense
Simple present tense
  affirmative statements,
    109-110, A12
  frequency, questions of,
    228-229
  how often questions, 228-229
  negative statements, 109-110
  non-action verbs and, 109
  on / ones and *it*, 137-138
  present progressive and,
    228-229
  pronunciation rules, A14
  short answers and, 117
  spelling rules, A14
  third-person singular, 110, A14
  this / that / these / those, 132
  wh- questions, 124-125
  yes / no questions, 117
    be, past tense, 28
    be, simple present tense
      of, 20-21
Singular count nouns. *See*
  Count nouns
Singular nouns,
  contractions and, 7
Some, 309-310, 317-318
Space, 258
Spelling rules
  plural nouns, A7

present progressive, A13

simple past tense of regular verbs, A15

simple present tense, A14

third-person singular affirmative, A14

Stative verbs. *See* Non-action verbs

Subject, defined, 66

Subject nouns, 6

Subject pronouns, 6, 194

contractions with, 7, 13

Suggestions

let's, 186-187

why don't we, 186-187

Superlative form

adjectives and, 424-425, A16

adverbs and, 424-425, A16

irregular, 425

one of the, 425

Temperature, A3

That

it and, 138

one / ones used after, 137-138

simple present tense, 132

The, 309-310, A10

Then, 145

There is / there are, 202-203

articles with, 210

numbers and quantifiers with, 209

yes / no questions, 202

and they are, 203

These, 132

Third-person singular

pronunciation rules for affirmative, 110, A14

spelling rules for affirmative, A14

This

it and, 138

one / ones used after, 137-138

simple present tense, 132

Those, simple present tense, 132

Time

clauses and use of *when*, 303-304

frequency expressions as

time markers, 229-230

markers

future, 280, 282

past, 28

prepositions of, and questions with *when* and *what*, 86-87

sequence markers, 258

simple past tense and past time markers, 151-152

writing organization and, 258

Titles, A4

To be born, 272

Too, plus adjective, 377-378

Too much / too many / too little / too few, 317, 319

Try, 245

Under, 52

Verbs

adverbs of frequency, 228-229

defined, 66

gerund following, 244-245

had better followed by base form, 406

imperatives and base form of, 186

infinitive following the, 244-245

irregular verbs, base forms and past-tense forms of common, A13

linking, 372

non-action, 236-237

non-action, and simple present tense with, 110

nouns following the, 244-245

present tense of be, 7, A11

simple past tense and irregular, 160

simple past tense and regular, 150-151, A12

Very plus adjective, 377, 379

Want, 245

Was / were, 160

Wasn't / weren't, 160, 264

Weather, 31-32

Well, 370-373

Wh- questions, form, simple past, 271

What questions, 70-77

be going to the future, 280

past tense of *be*, singular and plural subjects, 271

plus noun, 86-87

prepositions of time and, 86-87

present progressive and, 92-99

should, use of, 403-404

simple past tense, 167-169, 271-272

simple present tense, 124-125

subject at beginning of question, 125

third-person singular, use of, 125

will, 292-293

When, time clauses with, 303-304

When questions

be going to the future, 280

past tense of *be*, singular and plural subjects, 271

plus noun, 86-87

prepositions of time and, 86-87

should, use of, 403-404

simple past tense, 167-169, 271-272

simple present tense, 124-125

will, 292-293

Where questions, 70-77

be going to the future, 280

past tense of *be*, singular and plural subjects, 271

present progressive and, 92-99

should, use of, 403-404

simple past tense, 167-169, 271-272

simple present tense, 124-125

will, 292-293

While, 387

Whom questions
  be going to the future, 280
  object, questions about the, 125
  present progressive, 92-99
  simple past tense, 167-169, 271-272
  simple present tense, 124-125
  will, 292-293

Who questions, 70-77
  be going to the future, 280
  object, questions about the, 125
  past tense of *be*, singular and plural subjects, 271
  present progressive and, 92-99
  simple past tense, 167-169, 271-272
  simple present tense, 124-125
  subject, questions about the, 125
  third-person singular, use of, 125
  will, 292-293

Whose questions, possessive nouns / adjectives and, 78-84

Why don't we, 184-187

Why don't you, 184-187

Why questions
  be going to the future, 280
  past tense of *be*, singular and plural subjects, 271
  present progressive and, 92-99
  simple past tense, 167-169, 271-272
  simple present tense, 124-125
  will, 292-293

Will for the future, 291-293, A12, A17

Won't, 297

Worse, 362

Would like, 343-344, A17

Would you like, 343-344

Would you please, 343-344, A17

Yes / no questions
  be going to, 279-282
  can / could, use of, 328-329
  future, *be going to*, 279-282
  future, *will*, 291-293
  have to, 415-417
  past progressive, 386
  past tense of *be*, 28-29
  present progressive and, 56
  present tense of *be*, 20-21
  quantity, 317-319
  should, use of, 403
  simple past tense, 167-169, 263-264
    be, of, 263-264
  simple present tense, 117
    be, of, 20-21
  there is / there are, 202
  will, 291-293